The
End of
Life
Advisor

The
End of
Life
Advisor

Personal, Legal, and Medical
Considerations for a Peaceful,
Dignified Death

**Susan Dolan, RN, JD
Audrey Vizzard, RN, EdD**

KAPLAN

PUBLISHING

New York

This publication is designed to provide accurate and authoritative information in regard to the subject matter covered. It is sold with the understanding that the publisher is not engaged in rendering legal, medical, or other professional service. If legal or medical advice or other expert assistance is required, the services of a competent professional should be sought.

Published by Kaplan Publishing, a division of Kaplan, Inc.
1 Liberty Plaza, 24th Floor
New York, NY 10006   362.175

Printed in the United States of America

10 9 8 7 6 5 4 3 2 1

ISBN-13: 978-1-4277-9839-8

For hospice workers everywhere

Contents

INTRODUCTION

EARLY IN MY HOSPICE CAREER, a single event made me realize what a profound difference hospice care can make for patients and their loved ones. It happened when I visited a 90-year-old hospice patient in a nursing home and I was struck by the differences between her and a roommate, who was also 90 and dying.

The woman receiving hospice services was resting comfortably. The hospice staff had just visited to examine her, review medications, and give a shower, a shampoo, and a soothing massage. Reclining on clean sheets, in a fresh gown and wearing a little makeup, she seemed deeply relaxed.

In sharp contrast, her roommate appeared agitated. Groaning, she gripped the side rails on her bed. She was bloated, struggling to breathe, tethered to a feeding tube and an intravenous needle that delivered fluids and medications. Although she was unable to speak, the panic in her eyes clearly implored, "Please help me!"

I located a nurse and asked if this woman's family members were aware of hospice services. With resignation she shook her head and told me, "Her doctor doesn't believe in hospice. Instead, he recommended that the family agree to insertion of a feeding tube and continue aggressive medical treatments."

At that moment I felt an overwhelming urgency to take some action that would make a difference, to help educate anyone who would listen about how to achieve a peaceful, dignified death. All my experience as a nurse, healthcare attorney, hospice volunteer, community educator, and executive director of a hospice organization told me it was time to write this book.

As I began to write, I realized that I had shared and discussed most of my stories with my mother, Audrey. Early in this project, I asked her for feedback and she graciously offered, based on her years of experience as a nurse, psychologist, author, editor, and hospice volunteer. I knew I would benefit from her wisdom, so I asked if she would co-author this book with me. She agreed. This book is better because of Audrey. Although we have written it together, it is written in my narrative voice.

The End-of-Life Advisor is a simple guide to prepare you and your loved ones to die well. Written for every man and woman, young and old, patient or caregiver, whether you are living the last days or have years yet to go, you will find practical information and compassionate guidance to assist you in opening conversations with loved ones and in planning for excellent end-of-life care. In addition, attorneys, healthcare professionals, and financial advisors will gain an understanding of the more personal issues surrounding the end of life in order to better serve their clients.

Although this book is not a primer on wills and estates, it contains vital personal, legal, and medical information on how to achieve a peaceful, dignified death. Chapters 1 through 3 explain the importance of preparing legal documents for a smooth transition at the end of life and the necessity of discussing your wishes with loved ones. Chapters 4 through 7 describe the benefits of hospice, chapters 8 through 16 address the dying time, and chapters 17 and 18 discuss final arrangements. At the close of each chapter, you will find further considerations on important issues. The Afterword explains how to initiate difficult conversations about end-of-life care. Finally, the Prequel contains a brief history of events that led to the creation of *The End-of-Life Advisor.*

You are invited to draw close to the bedsides of dying people, listen to their words, and meet their families and caregivers. You will meet some heroes (and a few villains) and possibly experience a range of emotions that leap from love and compassion to anger and fear. However, before starting this journey, there remains a human impediment called denial to clear away.

"I don't want to achieve immortality through my work. I want to achieve it by not dying," said Woody Allen in his best neurotic whine. We may chuckle knowingly at his witticism, acknowledging it touches on the secret fears and chilling anxieties that surface in all of us when dealing with death.

Most of us choose to ignore death or at least stay as far away from it as possible. So unwelcome are thoughts of dying in our culture that we have developed a sturdy shield of denial to protect us from the knowledge and experience of what is a normal, natural life event.

Written in the hope of nurturing a new generation of courageous and informed trailblazers, this book seeks to lift the fog of denial surrounding death by describing what happens during the dying time, suggesting how to plan ahead, and encouraging informed choices that can lead to a peaceful departure.

Every story was inspired by real events and real people; however, most names have been changed. If some tales sound familiar to you, that may be because you are living them, or because they resonate with what is universal in the human condition.

The theme of planning runs throughout the book. You plan for births, parties, weddings, vacations, and retirement. Similarly, the best way to plan for an excellent death is to gather information ahead of time, determine and document your wants and needs, and discuss your wishes with those closest to you. Because ongoing conversations are an essential part of effective planning, attention must be focused on opportunities for such discussions. Each time the word "conversation" appears, it is italicized to remind you of yet another chance to inform loved ones of your wishes and to invite their input and understanding.

When planning and preparing for end-of-life care, it is important to understand a few realities about death and dying in the 21st century. If they have not already affected your life or the life of someone close to you, sooner or later they probably will. For example, did you ever consider how long you might live? The average caveman lived for about 20 years before being felled by another caveman's club or becoming lunch for a hungry hyena.

By the early 1900s life expectancy had doubled to about 40 years, but people still died quickly from killers like blood poisoning or pneumonia. With the advent of modern sanitation and antibiotics, along with great advances in medical technology, life expectancy today has grown to about 80 years.

There are downsides to such stunning progress. Death hasn't changed, but dying certainly has. In the past, death was usually relatively fast; today it is far more likely to be a costly, long, and drawn-out process. The "frail elderly" these days may live into their nineties and beyond, but they often suffer from multiple chronic diseases or are so physically and mentally impaired that they no longer recognize their loved ones. Their quality of life can be so diminished that, beyond breathing and a beating heart, they are barely alive.

Ten to 12 percent of the total healthcare budget is spent on end-of-life care. Twenty-seven to 30 percent of Medicare costs are incurred in the last year of life, and of this amount about 40 percent is spent during the last 30 days. Not only is our healthcare system mightily strained, but families are often faced with years of caregiving responsibilities and then left with overwhelming medical bills. Now that life can be artificially prolonged with ventilators and feeding tubes, thorny moral and ethical questions arise, such as, "When is enough *enough*?"

This book offers no easy answers to such dilemmas; instead, information is laid before you to heighten your awareness and invite you to discover your own best path.

PART ONE

THE WISDOM OF PLANNING AHEAD

CHAPTER I

Advance Directives

IN 1924 MY HUSBAND'S GRANDFATHER, V. J. Dolan, started the Chicago paint and coatings company that Steve and three of his brothers run today. During his professional life, Bill Dolan, Steve's father, ran the family business while mentoring his sons to take over. Through the years, I have admired the company slogan: *From the Start Consider the Finish.* It reminds me of hospice and excellent end-of-life care. Bill Dolan lived the motto, as you will read in this story.

When we were newlyweds, Steve asked if we could invite some Dolan relatives for dinner. After years of living as a single dad with his son Joe in a bachelor-sized condo, he was eager to open our new home to his family. "How many guests?" I asked faintly, fully aware that the Dolan clan numbered over 50 and that cooking was not my strong suit.

"Only 23," he promised.

Remain calm, I instructed myself. *Remember, for the Dolans, 23 is a small gathering.* Recalling the sage advice of a new sister-in-law (Call the caterer, 1-800-FEED-THE-DOLANS), I said to Steve in a sweet, newlywed voice, "Oh, sure, honey. Only 23?"

Actually, I looked forward to entertaining Gramps Dolan, the patriarch who delighted in any family event, grateful for an opportunity to sit quietly in the midst of his loved ones. At 85, he could barely see and he often fell. His enlarged thyroid gland prevented him from speaking clearly; he also suffered from severe hearing loss and a rapidly deteriorating body. Nevertheless, he struggled to stay engaged when his family gathered. From the depths of his favorite chair, he'd raise his right fist to his right shoulder, then swing it across his chest for emphasis proclaiming, "Wonderful, wonderful! Everything's just great!"

Laid back, humble, and soft spoken, he was a gentle husband and father of eleven children. His seven sons are gentlemen and each of his four daughters is like the girl next door. I'm not sure how he did it, but he had the ability to make each of us—daughters-in-law like me included—believe we were his favorite.

Early one morning, Steve answered an emergency call from his brother John, who was at their parents' home waiting for an ambulance to arrive. "Dad can't get up; he can't move or talk," he cried. The next call came from the emergency room. The admitting doctor wasted no words. "Your father has had a massive stroke. Your family needs to make a decision quickly about whether to put your father on a ventilator to help him breathe. With a ventilator, he will continue to live but probably never regain consciousness. Without a ventilator he could die today."

Knowing his father's wishes and with his mother's blessing, John requested that the doctor order hospice services and write a Do Not Resuscitate order (DNR). "No ventilator," he added. As he spoke, the Dolans were gathering. All eleven children and their spouses, from as far away as Arizona, would arrive at Bill's bedside by evening.

Gramps was the poster child for excellent end-of-life planning. He had decided how he wanted to be treated if he were ever in a position where he was ill and could not speak for himself. He had documented his wishes in advance and he had discussed those wishes with his family. There were many *conversations* over the years. He left no doubts: "Let nature take its course. No extraordinary measures. Keep me comfortable and let me go." Because of his careful planning, the family knew exactly what to do.

When Paula, the hospice nurse, arrived, she explained hospice and assured the family she would make Bill comfortable.

The whispers in the room ceased. Looking to Fran, Bill's wife, Paula asked, "Would you like hospice for your husband?"

With great dignity and in a strong, clear voice, Fran said, "Yes, and no extraordinary measures."

"But Mom," one son interrupted in growing realization of his impending loss, "we could keep Dad alive if we put him on a ventilator." A daughter added, "Aren't we really giving up all hope by admitting Dad to hospice?"

"Have you heard of the 'bridge to recovery' test?'" Paula asked. Every head shook no.

"Consider this," she continued. "Suppose you were in a serious accident, unconscious, with broken bones and internal injuries. You might undergo surgery, be placed on a ventilator to breathe for you, have a feeding tube inserted in your stomach, and receive medications through your veins. Of course, most people would want such aggressive treatments if their doctors offered a good chance for recovery. These temporary measures would serve as a bridge to your recovery until you could breathe on your own, swallow food and liquids, regain your strength, and get back on your feet. Nevertheless, in every life there comes a time, no matter what we do—find the best doctors and healthcare facility, provide lots of medications, arrange for surgery, chemotherapy and radiation, provide the love and prayers of family—when nothing can prevent someone we love from experiencing a physical death. There will be no bridge to recovery. Your father is at that point. He is dying."

Fran gently reminded her children that by accepting hospice she was honoring Bill's explicit wishes. Then, with a gaze that seemed directed to each of us at the same time, she said, "Dad gave us an invaluable gift; he told us exactly what to do in this situation: no extraordinary measures. We will abide by his wishes." Fran signed the hospice consents with the approval and support of her children. The room was still. We were aware that the life of our loved one hung feebly, briefly suspended in time.

What came next was hard to take. Congested, Bill struggled to inhale and exhale. Paula quickly relieved his discomfort with medications to dry up secretions and ease his respirations. Soon he was breathing more easily and everyone exhaled with him. In true Dolan form, the children gathered around their father's bed, reminiscing, telling jokes, laughing, and crying.

Bill slept comfortably through the night, watched over by siblings Mike and Mary. At 6:00 A.M. his breathing changed dramatically. With irregular breaths and lengthening pauses when he didn't breathe for 20 seconds or longer, it was clear the end was near. Once again, the Dolans assembled quickly.

As Fran held her husband's hand, one by one the children said their good-byes. Struggling to maintain composure, they identified themselves: Bill Jr., Dave, Mike, Mary, Steve, Bob, Jim, Denise, John, Beth, and Julie. Each in his or her own way thanked him for the family he founded and watched over, for having been a loving father, for all he had meant to them.

Last came his partner of 58 years. "Bill, this is Fran. Do you remember before we were married when your dad told you to treat me with kindness, the way he treated your mother? You did. Thank you for our wonderful life and for being so patient with my impatience. It's time to say good-bye. I love you." Almost imperceptibly, shortly after Fran's farewell, a single tear fell down Bill's cheek as he sighed his last breath at 6:30 A.M., less than 24 hours after suffering his stroke.

Because Gramps had an extraordinary work ethic that he passed on to his children, the family joked that he had allowed everyone to get some sleep and then died just in time for his sons to get back to work at V. J. Dolan.

Bill Dolan gave his family a great gift. He lived his company motto: *From the Start Consider the Finish.* By example, he taught his children how to live and how to die—lessons that will endure through the next generation and beyond. He reminded them that death is more than a medical occurrence; it is a personal, family, and spiritual event. Futile, aggressive, treatment would have robbed the family of a natural and deeply moving process. As much as they all loved Bill and continue to miss him, his children carry no burden of guilt, no regrets, none of the second-guessing that haunts so many families who are forced to make decisions when they don't know their loved one's wishes. Steve said, "I'm at peace because my father died well. Thanks to him, we were prepared and able to honor his wishes. We all have wonderful memories that continue to comfort us."

When it comes to death and dying, most people report they avoid *conversations* about their own demise and fail to make plans for it. Make your wishes clear, have *conversations* about what you want with your loved ones, and commit them to paper in an advance directive. An advance directive is simply a legal document you fill out in advance to direct loved ones about how you wish to be treated if you cannot speak on your own behalf. Identify who will make those decisions for you.

As Bill Dolan's story illustrates, the best time to have these *conversations* and complete your advance directive is before you become ill—before it's too late. Taking the time to plan and prepare now makes it reasonably certain that your wishes will be honored and last-minute conflicts between family members avoided. *From the start consider the finish.*

FURTHER CONSIDERATIONS ON
ADVANCE DIRECTIVES

There are two types of advance directives: a **living will** and a **power of attorney for healthcare**. Sometimes these documents are combined. A **living will** documents your wishes regarding medical treatment when you can no longer speak for yourself. **A power of attorney for healthcare** gives authority to another person to make healthcare decisions for you if you cannot express your own choices.

Without a decision maker (called a healthcare agent, proxy, surrogate, or representative) to articulate your wishes, they can be misinterpreted or, more likely, ignored in favor of futile aggressive treatment. This happens is because many healthcare professionals are extremely hesitant to withhold or discontinue life-sustaining treatment.

Complete a living will and a power of attorney for healthcare, choose the best decision maker, and open *conversations* about your wishes. Select one or two alternate agents in case your primary agent becomes unavailable.

Factors to consider when choosing a healthcare agent include:

- Will the agent put personal preferences aside and follow your wishes?

- Is the agent willing to pursue your wishes aggressively, even against opposition from others, including doctors?

- Is the agent able to understand medical information?

- Is the agent geographically close or available so he or she can be present when decisions must be made?

Keep originals and many copies of your advance directives in a safe place in your home for easy access. Give copies to your healthcare agent, alternate agents, loved ones, doctor, lawyer, and any healthcare facility you are admitted to. Keep a card in your wallet or purse stating you have an advance directive, where the documents are located, and the names and phone numbers of your healthcare agents.

For more information about advance directives, see Appendixes E and G.

CHAPTER 2

The Importance of Conversations about End-of-Life Care

"HE DID *WHAT?*"

"Ms. Miller's son Bruce punched his sister in the face!" the breathless social worker called to tell me. "A nurse called the police; they arrested Bruce and rushed his sister Tracy to the emergency room. At least she was already in the hospital! He was released and she's patched up. They've settled down now and he's promised to behave. Can you come right away? Oh, and I should warn you, he's a puncher, but she's a screecher."

Once reunited, the siblings immediately reopened their argument about whether their 88-year-old mother, who was dying of dementia and refusing all food and fluids, should receive hospice care.

"The last one in creates the biggest stink," quipped a geriatric doctor. Bruce had arrived from a distant state only the day before. Like many out-of-towners who haven't seen a loved one for a long time, the shock of viewing a shrunken body or the patient's inability to communicate with or even recognize the visitor prompts demands like, "Do something! I want to talk to the doctor!" or "Can't you (stupid people) see she's dying?"

Bruce was true to form. "Hospice is a death sentence. Hospice kills people," he declared angrily. "The nurses should be feeding our mother and helping her get better!"

Tracy, on the other hand, had been present at her mother's bedside every day. Over a period of weeks, observing her steady decline, she came to understand and accept that her mother was suffering and had no reasonable hope for recovery. "Well, I think we should get hospice so she can be comfortable and die naturally," Tracy screeched with volume equal to her brother's.

The basic disagreement between these siblings is one repeated all too often: an elderly parent, ill for years, has never completed an advance directive. The parent may not even know what an advance directive is. Neither they nor their children ever considered a *conversation* about end-of-life care wishes. Then comes a stroke or some disease that incapacitates them mentally. From then on, it's guesswork for the family. Matters become more complicated when loved ones live far away, there is a history of poor communication, or family feuds divide siblings into warring camps.

"Bruce, it's time to let Mom go," Tracy pleaded.

"You say let her go; I say that's killing her. You always were bossy!" he glowered. It was clear they disagreed about everything, not only about what each believed their mother would want. Bruce's face grew redder as Tracy's screech climbed another decibel. "You always were a bully!" she responded. Yelling appeared to be the major form of communication in this family.

We were getting nowhere fast. Hoping to defuse the growing tension and find some common ground for negotiation, I took a deep breath and said, "Do you really want to continue fighting over your mother's body? You may never agree, but could each of you rise above yourself, put your disagreements on hold, come together, and focus on her needs?

"You could spend this little bit of precious time with her, hold her hand, talk to her, and tell her how much you love her. Speak of your happy memories; thank her for all she's done. Even if she doesn't seem to hear you, she knows you are with her. Her awareness is greater than her ability to respond."

Noting that Bruce was struggling to rethink his position, I asked, "What do you think your mother would say if she could sit up in bed right now and speak to you?" Tracy, who had been admirably silent for a few minutes, broke in before Bruce had a chance to reply.

"I know," she said. "I think she'd say, 'Would you want to live like this?' and she'd yell like when we were kids, 'All right, Miss Big-mouth and Mr. Muscles, stop fighting, or I'll tell your father when he gets home!'" Then in a quieter voice, she added, "I think Mom would say, 'Why would I want to continue like this, flat on my back, unable to move, to walk or talk, with no reasonable hope that I'll get better? Please keep me comfortable, love me, and let me go.'"

Bruce stood up to leave. "I need more time to think about this. Let's meet tomorrow morning and we'll settle things," he said in a thought-ful tone.

I'd like to tell you that Bruce returned to agree to hospice care for his mother, but Mrs. Miller died that night. In retrospect I think Bruce was shocked and dismayed to see his mother's decline, her tenuous hold on life, and her inability to recognize his presence. Bruce fell back into a familiar pattern of disagreeing with anything his sister wanted.

Sometimes such deathbed battles are not so much about the dying person's wishes as they are a reenactment of old resentments and ancient rivalries. Bitter fights arise when adults under pressure regress to child-hood sibling roles: the smart one, the dumb one, the bossy one, the martyr, the peacemaker. In the emotional turmoil of the dying time, rather than address the issue, they blame each other, the doctors, the nursing staff, or hospice for not doing more.

Without prior *conversations* with everyone who may be in the patient's room at the end of life, including out-of-town relatives, it is unrealistic to expect families to come to a quick, unified decision that satisfies everyone.

A relative living down the street may be as much an "out-of-towner" as Bruce was. Whether the distance is one block or a thousand miles, sometimes a wide chasm splits a family.

Consider the brothers Josh and Sam, who lived in the same city. Reluctantly Josh had secured a temporary restraining order to prevent Sam from entering their mother's house because every time he did, a battle erupted over their mother's care.

"Oh, I don't want to do this," Josh moaned to the hospice nurse. He was trembling with anxiety knowing that he must leave for a court hearing in less than an hour where he would face his intimidating older brother. What started as a tense disagreement over who should make healthcare decisions for their mother had escalated into an ugly legal battle. Sam planned to convince the court to appoint him as their mother's guardian, alleging that Josh was an unfit caregiver. Josh was torn between staying at his dying mother's bedside and appearing in court.

Josh never married or left home. He had always lived with his mother, and years ago he had become her full-time caregiver. Five months before, on the advice of her doctor, Josh admitted their mother to hospice care over Sam's protests. Sam demanded that their mother be hospitalized so a feeding tube could be surgically inserted and more aggressive treatments pursued. Josh refused.

A few days earlier, as his mother slipped in and out of consciousness, she had told Josh, "I know that I am dying. I can't remember things clearly now, but I trust you to do everything I asked you to do." Years before she had completed an advance directive naming Josh as her healthcare agent. Over the years she and Josh had many *conversations* about her wishes. In particular she had asked for hospice care and no extraordinary measures at the end of her life. She had neglected to tell Sam of her wishes, she had failed to invite his input, and she had not given him a copy of her advance directive document—possibly out of fear that he would contest her decisions.

Only minutes before a shaken Josh was scheduled to leave for court, his mother died, rendering the legal dispute a moot point but leaving two bitterly alienated brothers.

"Who will be in the room?" is the question all of us need to ask as we begin to plan and prepare for end-of-life care. If Sam's mother had explained to him why she chose Josh as her healthcare agent (because he was always with her) and had asked Sam to support Josh in this role, it is likely that he would have honored her wishes.

Dr. Hill, once a prominent anesthesiologist, became a patient in the intensive care unit of the hospital where he'd practiced for over 30 years. After a massive stroke, he was unresponsive, on a ventilator, fed through a feeding tube in his stomach, and receiving medications through an intravenous needle (IV). His colleagues recalled that throughout the years he often had said, "If I have no hope for recovery, push me off a cliff in my wheelchair." After several weeks with no improvement, his doctors agreed that Dr. Hill should have hospice care.

Immediately a problem arose. Dr. Hill's wife, June, had been his healthcare agent, as he was hers. "June is not only my wife, she is my life," he often said fondly. June had died unexpectedly the year before he became ill. Any one of his many friends would have been willing to serve as his healthcare agent; however, in his grieving, the normally conscientious Dr. Hill had neglected to update his advance directive. There was no second agent listed.

According to the state surrogacy law, Dr. Hill's nephew, George, was next in line as a medical decision maker. A social worker tracked down George, who was difficult to reach by telephone, surly, and seemingly indifferent to assuming any responsibility for his uncle. "If I'm not in the will, forget it," he said.

Dr. Hill's friends believed that he would have been appalled to learn that his black sheep nephew was asked to make healthcare decisions for him. He died in the intensive care unit with a social worker still trying to find a surrogate for him.

The best way to avoid such outcomes when people can no longer state their own wishes is for every competent adult to assume personal responsibility to make decisions and open a *conversation* with anyone likely to be in the room at the end of life. The next step is to complete, then regularly review advance directives. (Many attorneys recommend reviewing these documents on one's birthday and after a major life event such as a serious illness, marriage, divorce, or death.) Identify and educate at least two agents about your wishes, and give copies of the directive to your doctor, lawyer, agents, and anyone likely to be in the room.

FURTHER CONSIDERATIONS ON SURROGACY

If you do not have an advance directive and you are not able to make healthcare choices for yourself, a majority of states allow a **surrogate decision maker to make decisions for you.** The healthcare surrogate is chosen in order of priority; in addition, the surrogate's willingness and ability to serve as a medical decision maker is considered.

State law governs the order of priority. In Illinois, for example, the order is:

- Guardian of the person
- Spouse
- Any adult son or daughter
- Either parent
- Any adult sibling
- Any adult grandchild
- A close friend
- Guardian of the estate

Because a surrogate may not be the person you would have chosen to make your healthcare decisions, he or she may make decisions that do not agree with your end-of-life choices. *Therefore the importance of completing an advance directive and educating your healthcare agent about your wishes cannot be overstressed.*

To learn more about the law in your state regarding surrogate decision makers, contact your state's hospice, bar, medical, or hospital association.

CHAPTER 3

The Do Not Resuscitate
Order (DNR)

O N A THURSDAY NIGHT, our elderly neighbor Grace was not feeling well. That day she had refused her medications and break-
fast. When she tried to get out of bed, she fell. Family members called
Grace "Kitty Cat" because after a quick trip to the hospital, she had
always bounced back from one or more of her many ailments, like a cat
with nine lives.

This time was different. Julia, Grace's daughter and longtime caregiver, knew that something was very wrong when she called me early
Friday morning. "Susan," she said, "I think my mother is really dying
this time. She's talking to me but it seems hard for her to breathe. I've
put a call in to her doctor, but could you come right now?"

As I hurriedly dressed and raced across the street, I thought about
Grace and Julia. At 97, Grace was still stunning. Always perfectly
groomed, she wore beautifully coordinated outfits accented by her
trademark powder pink gloves. Pure white hair rose high above her head
in a beehive style from the 1960s. If that hairdo didn't get your attention, her cherry red lipstick from the forties surely would.

Although Julia credited Grace's impossibly smooth skin to two daily
slatherings of Lady Esther skin cream, everyone knew the real secret to
Grace's longevity was Julia's loving care. Grace's goal was to travel to
New York with her doctor on her 100th birthday, at which time her

picture would appear on the Smucker's jar and she'd collect congratulations from Willard Scott on the *Today* show.

Every day Grace reclined in her favorite chair before a huge picture window. She smiled and waved to walkers, bicyclists, and passing cars. As the self-appointed neighborhood watchdog, she sat ready to take a bite out of crime on our sleepy street. Once while visiting, I was surprised at her panoramic view of our home. Her window was like a movie screen, and Grace had the best seat in the house.

I smiled, finally realizing how Julia knew more about my stepson Joe's girlfriends than either his father or I did. Private eye Grace kept watch and reported what clothes the girls wore or didn't wear, what model cars they drove, and how many times Joe hugged and kissed them as they came and went.

As I stepped into her bedroom that Friday, it was immediately apparent to me that although she was fully conscious, Grace was dying. She weakly acknowledged my presence with a barely raised hand.

Grace had completed an advance directive and was well aware of the benefits of hospice. Several years earlier, Julia's husband had died in their home with the support of a hospice team. Knowing that Julia had prepared Grace for my visit, I anticipated my role would be a simple matter of confirming Grace's wishes and starting the hospice admission process so she could become comfortable as quickly as possible. However, before I could begin, Julia whispered to me, "She wants hospice but getting the DNR might be an issue."

A Do Not Resuscitate order (DNR) is a physician's written instruction to medical personnel not to attempt cardiopulmonary resuscitation (CPR) if a patient's heart stops beating or if they cease breathing. Home-based hospice patients are advised to post the DNR form on their refrigerator so emergency medical personnel have immediate access to the document. The DNR protects hopelessly ill patients from futile and aggressive treatment in the event that a neighbor or a family member panics and calls 911 at the time of death.

For someone who is hopelessly ill, a DNR is really a protective order. Contrary to what fictional TV medical dramas depict, CPR is almost never successful for the frail elderly and terminally ill. A better name for a DNR would be an Allow a Natural Death order.

If dying patients want hospice care and they understand that the DNR actually protects them at the end of life, completing a DNR is not an issue. However, if a seriously ill person or the family resists a DNR, as is often the case, it's usually because the realities of CPR and the benefits of the Do Not Resuscitate order have not been explained or comprehended thoroughly.

Julia was direct. "Mom, Susan is here to talk about hospice. Is that what you want?" Grace nodded and whispered, "Yes, I want to stay here . . . in my bed."

Then I stepped in to ask Grace about the DNR. Because in the past she had always chosen to go to the hospital for aggressive treatment, I wanted to be certain she understood she would avoid a trip to the emergency room by signing a DNR.

"Grace, when your heart stops beating and you stop breathing, it's my understanding you want to let nature take its course so you can die at home. Is that right?"

"Yes." She nodded.

I repeated, "The paramedics will not be called when your heart stops because our goal is to keep you comfortable and allow you to die peacefully here. Right?"

Grace looked me straight in the eye and said clearly, "Wrong! That's what I want."

"What do you mean?" I asked.

"I want to go to the hospital," Grace replied.

Julia and I looked at each other with that uh-oh look. At the same moment both of us realized that Grace didn't have a clue about what the paramedics must do if they responded to a 911 call when she died. Grace's tiny, 102-pound body almost certainly would not survive the trauma of chest compressions, electric shock to the heart, artificial breathing tubes, and powerful drugs. Even if she did live, possible brain injury from oxygen deprivation, broken ribs, bruises, internal injuries, and placement on a ventilator would most likely be her fate.

"Mom doesn't understand that this time is different. After each previous trip to the hospital she came home again, feeling better," Julia said as she moved to her mother's bedside and took her hand. Simply, honestly, but graphically, Julia explained the likely consequences of CPR and hospitalization while gently repeating that she would honor whatever choice her mother made.

Then she was blunt. "Mom, you always told us that you wanted to stay home with hospice care at the end. If we call the paramedics when your heart stops beating, that won't happen. They will take you to the emergency room. The DNR protects you; it's consistent with your choice for hospice." Grace closed her eyes as though pondering, then opened them and nodded. "Julia, sign it for me," she said.

Now the hospice team leapt into action like a MASH unit, calling Grace's doctor, dispatching the admission nurse, and arranging for oxygen, medication, and a hospital bed to be delivered to the house—all within a few hours.

Grace's story illustrates the importance of a Do Not Resuscitate order. Because of the DNR, Grace avoided a visit to the emergency room that she did not want and would not have benefited from. Instead, a team of end-of-life professionals came to her, quickly, providing care for her and emotional support for her family.

Grace died the next day after slipping in and out of consciousness. Julia and her family kept vigil in the comfort of their own home.

FURTHER CONSIDERATIONS ON DO NOT RESUSCITATE ORDERS

Grace's story makes a compelling case for the necessity of a Do Not Resuscitate order (DNR) for seriously ill persons who do not want cardiopulmonary resuscitation (CPR). If you or a loved one are in a similar situation, ask your doctor to complete a DNR, then tape it to your refrigerator door. If you reside in a healthcare facility or are in the hospital, inquire to make sure your DNR is in your medical chart and that staff know your wishes. As added insurance, one elderly woman hired a tattoo artist to inscribe "DO NOT RESUSCITATE!" across her chest.

Remember too that your physician must complete your DNR. It is not enough that you have an advance directive (power of attorney for healthcare and living will) in place. You must also have a separate Do Not Resuscitate order written by a doctor or other authorized person.

Finally, remember that a DNR order may always be revoked if you change your mind.

PART TWO

THE BENEFITS OF HOSPICE

CHAPTER 4

Hospice

HOSPICE IS A PHILOSOPHY of care rooted in the age-old tradition of offering comfort and shelter to weary and sick travelers. Dame Cicely Saunders, a nurse, social worker, and physician, founded the first modern hospice in 1967 in England. "We do not have to cure to heal," Dame Cicely said as she addressed the emotional, spiritual, and medical needs of dying patients and their families. In 1974 the first hospice in the United States opened in New Haven, Connecticut. In the early 1980s Congress established the Medicare hospice benefit to pay for comprehensive hospice care wherever a patient resides.

Contacting hospice for a free consultation is not a commitment. Instead, it is an opportunity to gather information and learn more about end-of-life care options. For example, most people do not know that hospice services funded by Medicare are available for people who have six months or less to live. Since no one has a crystal ball for predicting exact life expectancy, if a patient lives longer than six months, hospice care can continue with a doctor's recertification.

Following is a summary covering the highlights of hospice care.

- Hospice treats the patient, not the illness; the focus is on care, not cure.

- The hospice team takes a holistic approach to care by addressing the physical, emotional, and spiritual needs of patients and their loved ones. Team members are sensitive to cultural differences. They take the time necessary to work with patients and families to achieve mutual trust and understanding.

- Hospice staff care for patients in the home, the hospital, long-term care facilities, assisted and independent living facilities, and inpatient and residential hospice facilities.

- Hospice cares for patients with life-threatening illnesses like cancer. Other conditions include heart disease, kidney disease, lung disease, Parkinson's disease, coma, stroke, dementia, and other age-related illnesses.

- Hospice care is paid for by Medicare (Part A), Medicaid, and most private insurance providers. Many hospices also provide care for patients who do not have insurance.

- Services include visits from the hospice interdisciplinary team, medications related to the terminal illness, and equipment and supplies approved by hospice.

- Hospice staff are available 24 hours a day. Staff members typically do not remain in the home around the clock but do make intermittent visits as needed to provide care and to support and educate patients and loved ones.

- A patient's primary physician may remain the attending doctor throughout the course of hospice care. The hospice staff and attending physician then work together to provide care that best suits each patient's individual needs.

- A patient may discontinue hospice at any time and then be read-mitted at a later date if hospice admission criteria are met.

- A doctor's order is required to receive hospice services. If your doctor doesn't agree that hospice is indicated, you are free to seek a second opinion.

- Hospice care for children is a rapidly expanding service in hospice programs throughout the nation.

- Thousands of hospice programs exist in the United States. For questions to consider asking when choosing a hospice and for more information on how to select a hospice, see Appendixes E and F.

Although hospice is a comprehensive, highly successful program, it is not perfect. Bad weather can delay visit times, cars break down, staff members get sick, misunderstandings occur. Keep the lines of communication open if you have any questions or concerns.

When humorist Art Buchwald's kidneys were failing, reluctantly he agreed to start dialysis. Before he began, however, he suffered terrible pain from blood clots, and his right leg was amputated. Three times a week for five hours at a time he was connected to a "washing machine" that filtered his blood and removed toxins from his body. He believed he was living his final days. After a few treatments, he made two decisions. The first was to stop dialysis. The second was to accept hospice care in full knowledge that patients with kidney failure who discontinue dialysis rarely live longer than a few weeks.

Despite all medical predictions, Art didn't die; he began to get better, so much better that he discontinued hospice care. "I'm practicing now not being dead," he announced. Delighted with the attention he received, reveling in the company of his family and friends, he lived on for another five months. He accepted his unexpected postscript to life with humor and gratitude. "I've been on standby for heaven, but my plane was canceled," he explained.

Art Buchwald was not the only patient to improve with hospice care. It's not unusual for patients to feel better after entering hospice simply because of the loving care lavished upon them by a team that attends to physical health, emotional needs, and spiritual well-being. Moreover, patients already in a weakened state who stop radiation or chemotherapy or discontinue multiple medications often feel better quickly because they are freed from the side effects of such treatments.

When you feel good, appetite often returns. Eat more, and energy picks up. With such benefits, it's not unusual for a dying person to recover an interest in living. When patients perk up, hospice workers often remind loved ones it's wise to wait a while to determine if the improvement is temporary or long term.

"Never again will you hear me complain about all the paperwork we have to do when we admit someone who has only hours to live," promised Lucia, a longtime hospice secretary and a veteran complainer about the stack of paperwork that accompanies every admission.

"Oh?" I raised my eyebrows.

"I never understood why admitting someone to hospice at the very end of life made any sense. So much paperwork here in the office, not to mention all the time the field staff puts in assessing patient and family needs and then starting care. Hours and hours of admission paperwork when you know the patient is likely to die so soon." Lucia paused. "Now I get it."

"What happened to change your mind?"

Tears began as Lucia continued, "This weekend my dearest friend, Olga, was hospitalized. She's been fighting cancer for years, then everything went south at once. When I visited her on Saturday she was screaming, writhing in pain, held down by restraints. I was horrified. Her sister Ana had been taking good care of her, but she was burned out and panicking. When Ana told me the doctors said there was nothing else they could do, she collapsed and sobbed, 'I can't do this anymore.'

"I suggested hospice. Olga agreed immediately, pleading, 'Just do something! Do something!' Within hours of her admission to hospice, she was made comfortable with a combination of effective medications. Her restraints were gone and she was sleeping soundly.

"Olga died peacefully early the next morning. The hospice nurse called the social worker, who supported Ana and helped her make funeral plans. I don't know what they would have done without hospice."

FURTHER CONSIDERATIONS ON
CONTACTING HOSPICE

If you have questions about hospice, the time to call is now. The number one comment on hospice family satisfaction surveys is "I wish I had known about hospice sooner."

If you request a hospice consultation and your doctor seems reluctant, you are free to seek a second opinion. It is important that your physician support your end-of-life care choices. Hospice can help you open a *conversation* with your doctor or assist you in locating hospice-friendly physicians.

CHAPTER 5

Laughter Is Good Medicine

ALTHOUGH THERE IS NOTHING FUNNY ABOUT DYING, some of the events that unfold during the dying process are genuinely humorous.

My friend Juanita is a hospice "lifer," a person so dedicated to hospice ideals that she enjoys speaking to community groups to educate others. She's in high demand because she adds humor to her presentations, thereby easing some of the fear and mystery about end-of-life care.

Among her many gifts, Juanita is an expert hairstylist. She cuts her own hair, my hair, and the locks of many other hospice workers. She even makes hair jokes. After going out on call in the middle of the night, she reported to work early the next morning, sighing, "I'm so tired my hair hurts!"

For special occasions, Juanita will style a patient's hair. Once she volunteered to create a fashionable look for Mary, a 93-year-old hospice patient for what would clearly be her last birthday party. Everyone in the nursing home where she lived was invited.

After the nursing assistant showered and shampooed Mary and dressed her in a stylish new pink pantsuit, Juanita took over, humming happily, blow-drying and brushing, as she moved behind the wheelchair. In her cheerful singsong voice, Juanita gushed, "Oh Mary, there's nothing like a good blow job in the morning, is there?"

Instantly the happy buzz in the room fell silent. Mortified at what had slipped out of her mouth, Juanita turned off the blow-dryer and stammered, "Oh, oh, oh, I'm so sorry, Mary. I didn't mean to say that!"

Slowly turning her head to look up at Juanita, Mary chuckled and said, "Oh honey, that's so funny! We don't get to talk dirty around here very often."

Juanita laughed so hard that she cried along with the delighted Mary, who hadn't had this much fun in a long time. Needless to say, this story remains a favorite hospice tale. Choosing her audiences carefully, Juanita repeats her story to illustrate that the very old, the dying, and just about everyone benefits from laughter.

Many patients cling to a zest for life and a sense of humor that endear them to hospice workers. Lorraine was one of those people. The hospice team adored her. Whenever I think of her, I can hear her deep smoker's laugh, feel the lush velvets of her gowns, and see her jewel-tone brocades from her former life. The fabrics she favored were ones you might choose for drapes or a sofa, only on her they looked elegant.

I met Lorraine late in her illness. Like many cancer patients, she had survived for years with surgery, chemotherapy, and radiation, but when such treatments were no longer helpful, she and her husband, Jeb, decided it was time to seek hospice care.

When I enter a home for the first time, I'm always drawn to family photographs displayed on a table or hung on a wall. Often faded and covered with a film of dust, they tell the story of lives past and children long since grown. Here's a pretty young girl clutching a high school diploma; there is a serious young man in military attire. A smiling couple in wedding finery look confidently into the future.

What captured my attention upon entering Lorraine's bedroom was a large, ornately framed photograph of herself: a beautiful young blonde, hair cascading from beneath a rakishly angled cowboy hat, eyebrows plucked to a thin line, lipstick bold and dark. Looking over her shoulder with a challenging, mischievous glance, she seemed to say, "Look at me; see who I was. Just remember, I'm still that person."

In her prime Lorraine was a singer and actress. A drama queen, she delighted in entertaining us with outrageous stories that always starred her in highly improbable adventures. Also, she offered us lots of advice such as, "When life gives you lemons, put them in your bra," and "Men are like linoleum; if you lay them right, you can walk all over them."

When she could summon the strength, Lorraine often asked the hospice staff to dress her in some ornate dressing gown that hung loosely on her emaciated frame. One day she asked me and her nurse to take her to Kmart, which had become her favorite store. After dressing her in a plum-colored velvet evening wrap and her favorite stiletto heels, we picked her up and carried her to the car. A few minutes later we plunked her into a wheelchair for a whirlwind tour of Kmart. The only purchase Lorraine made that day was Clairol semipermanent blond hair color. "I'm semipermanent," she laughed.

Humor is often a welcome guest when hospice workers come together for staff meetings or when they gather informally to share knowledge and exchange stories. Consider Lia, a nurse in a hospice unit, who tells a story that left her on the brink of a panic attack. As a funeral director removed the body of a recently deceased woman, he stopped at the nurses' station to pick up what he thought was the woman's small black bag of belongings. On the way out, he thanked the unit secretary for gathering her dress, false teeth, and a photo he'd requested to guide him in preparing her hair and makeup for the wake. Then he waved good-bye.

Unknown to Lia, the secretary had mistakenly handed over Lia's black gym bag containing her swimsuit and goggles. You can guess what happened next. Lia called the funeral home, praying that the deceased woman's family had not yet arrived. Before she could explain the mix-up, the funeral director chuckled and said, "I think we have something of yours."

After a sigh of relief, Lia laughed and said, "What did you think when you opened the bag? That she wanted burial at sea?"

Anyone who gets up in the morning, brushes their teeth, and goes outside is looking for trouble, someone once told me. This warning is especially true for hospice professionals. They never know what the day may bring, but they always welcome laughter.

When people laugh together, bonds form. Think of your own experience and the times when shared laughter brought you closer to other people. Humor has many expressions. There is the laughter that erupts when you recognize something amusing in another's comments, or the laughter that accompanies a flood of gratitude when one narrowly averts some mishap, as in a near-miss accident. Shared laughter can also ease the difficulty of absorbing bad news or defuse the tension of an escalating disagreement.

Laughter in the sickroom lightens the mood for everyone. Contrary to the view that dictates that others should be somber and silent in the presence of a dying person, bringing laughter or even just a smile to a dying person is a priceless gift.

Laughter and humor go a long way toward easing the sadness and stress that accompany so much of hospice work. Throughout this book you will meet many other instances where laughter greased the wheels, eased the way, and saved the day for people struggling with death and dying.

FURTHER CONSIDERATIONS ON LAUGHTER

Laughter is powerful medicine. Laughing can help decrease stress, control pain, relax muscles, increase circulation, elevate mood, increase energy, improve brain function, lower blood pressure, boost the immune system, enhance learning, and bring joy.

CHAPTER 6

The Hospice Team

Meet Divina, hospice nurse. She taught me much of what I know about the heart and art of hospice. Divina is fiercely devoted to her patients and outspoken on their behalf. Patients and their families adore her for her tireless pursuit of quality end-of-life care. I frequently remind her that she cannot retire until she sees me out.

Divina embodies the finest qualities of the best hospice nurses. Smart, intuitive, and compassionate, she has the strength of an ox and a dry sense of humor worthy of a stand-up comedian. She knows the healing power of laughter and uses it generously to release tension for patients and staff.

Once I overheard a conversation in the nurse's lounge. A new staff member, Meera, asked Divina how long she thought her patient had to live.

"I told you guys, I don't have a crystal ball and I don't get emails from God; however, your patient does appear to be on the banana peel," Divina answered with a straight face.

"On the banana peel?" the fledgling asked, thoroughly confused.

"You know, in the shortest checkout line at the supermarket?"

"Divina! Stop!" interrupted Tim, the unit manager. "This is Meera's first day. Give her a break." He turned to Meera. "What Divina means is that your patient will likely die very soon. While it's difficult to forecast the exact time of death, there are many predictable signs and symptoms that help us know when death is near." Divina apologized to Meera and promptly took her aside for a short course on the signs of impending death, thereby securing another admiring fan. The hospice team includes the following people:

Nurse and Certified Nursing Assistant. Consider Gennie, the hospice nurse, and Iris, the certified nursing assistant (CNA), who attended my stepfather, Joe, in his last days. The hospice nurse and CNA work as a team. The nurse assesses patient needs, creates a care plan, and supervises the CNA, who provides personal care including bed baths, showers, shaving, and skin care.

My mother told me, "We had no sooner signed up for hospice than this gorgeous creature, sporting a mop of curly hair, arrived. She swept into our bedroom wearing a wildly flowered, floor-length full skirt. Taking one look at the situation, she smiled at Joe, and said, 'How would you like a delightful warm shower?' He nodded weakly.

"For days, Joe had been too feeble to turn himself in bed or to stand alone. I'd been unable to bathe him properly, and a shower clearly was in order. Gennie and Iris slid this six-foot-six man out of bed and into a wheelchair, and rolled him into the shower, all in about thirty seconds. Gennie hiked up her swirling skirt to reveal a pair of ankle-length chartreuse tights, then climbed into the shower with Joe. Gently she sprayed him with warm water, soaped him down, and sprayed him again. As she patted him dry, Iris stripped the bed and remade it with clean sheets and cushiony, absorbent pads. I stood by in helpless wonder.

"As they moved Joe back to bed, Gennie suggested I play a CD of his favorite music. As the strains of a piano concerto filled the room, Gennie and Iris massaged him with their soothing salves, speaking softly, explaining everything they did. Before the CD ended, Joe was deeply asleep and I fell in love with hospice."

In another case, early one morning a hospice nurse named Maria and an aide named Pam quietly slipped into their patient Camilla's room in what turned out to be the last day of her life. The day before, after weeks of watching her continue to decline, the family had followed Camilla's previously stated wishes and agreed that the time had come to remove her ventilator. Shortly the family would gather to say their last good-byes.

Camilla's head had been shaved in preparation for what turned out to be unsuccessful brain surgery. Her formerly dyed red hair was now a stubbly white crew cut. "Without her red hair and fingernails and lips to match, my mother looks like someone we don't know," Camilla's son sadly remarked to Maria.

Maria and Pam got to work in preparation for the rest of the family's arrival. Given the circumstances, they bent the rules and colored Camilla's hair her familiar red. Then they bathed her and exchanged her hospital gown for her favorite leopard-print nightgown. They manicured her nails, put a bit of blush on her cheeks, and carefully applied lipstick. When Camilla's children saw her, they laughed and they cried. Mom was back, if only for a little while.

Hospice nurses and aides in action are true professionals. Whatever their mood, their level of fatigue, or the pressure of their own problems, when they approach a dying person, they seem to transform. Whether gently stroking the bald head of an old homeless man and crooning softly, "Everything will be all right," or embracing the parents of a dying child, these workers know what to do and how to do it.

Social Worker. Typically a social worker will visit soon after a patient's admission to hospice to explore family dynamics, financial and emotional burdens, and other concerns including advance directives and funeral arrangements.

Mollie, a longtime hospice social worker, actually threw herself across the body of a dead woman to prevent paramedics from performing CPR and removing the body to the hospital for further attempts at resuscitation. She kept the paramedics at bay by refusing to get up and reminding them that the patient had been in hospice care, was dead, and had a DNR order, which, unfortunately, no one could locate in the tiny, cluttered senior complex apartment.

This is what had happened. Unable to get an answer at her sick friend's door, a concerned neighbor panicked and called 911. Realizing that the resident had either died or needed immediate assistance, an alert clerk at the front desk called hospice. Luckily Mollie was in the neighborhood and arrived just before the paramedics. Once called, expect emergency medical personnel to attempt resuscitation and remove the patient to the hospital to be treated or pronounced dead unless a DNR is present.

"Get up, lady, or we're calling the cops," a paramedic ordered Mollie.

"Go ahead." Mollie refused to budge. By the time the police arrived, she had spotted the DNR form under the kitchen table and everything was quickly resolved.

Mollie's story illustrates that whatever the challenge—be it securing funds for an airplane ticket for a needy family member, seeking leave for a military person to return home, or locating a distant relative or a misplaced DNR—social workers usually find a way. Mollie's story also illustrates why it's important to keep a copy of the DNR on the refrigerator door where anyone can find it.

Physician. Hospice physicians take on many responsibilities, including leading team members in developing an individual plan of care for each patient, assessing special needs, ordering treatments, managing physical and psychological symptoms, and consulting with other physicians.

Hospice doctors are experts in pain and symptom management. In one instance a nurse was unable to relieve a woman's pain early on a Sunday morning. The nurse called the hospice doctor, who arrived shortly to find her on the floor with the writhing patient, rocking her as she would a sick child. After assessing the situation, the doctor immediately ordered a new combination of medications. Then he helped the nurse get up, and the two of them put the patient back to bed. The medicine arrived promptly and quickly eased the woman's suffering.

"He made me feel as though I was the only person in the room" is the way one patient described her hospice physician. "No overbooking, no rushed 15-minute time slot for me!" she said.

Hospice doctors know it's the little things that make a big difference. "Doc, the only drink I want, the only one that doesn't taste awful to me is root beer," said one elderly man. The doctor disappeared and returned to personally deliver an ice-cold root beer to his grateful patient. Then, in large print, he wrote an order on the chart: "Root beer with every meal." When the man died peacefully a few days later, the doctor was asked to verify the cause of death. "Death by root beer?"

Hospice patients are free to keep their own attending physician. When this happens, the patient's doctor and the hospice doctor consult back and forth. For example, when a nursing home patient was unable to travel to the hospital to have uncomfortable abdominal fluid removed, the hospice doctor traveled to the patient to perform the procedure.

Chaplain. Hospice chaplains are a special breed. They embrace all denominations and honor all spiritual paths. They offer support to anyone who desires their presence, following the lead of patients and family members. They will pray silently or aloud, read scripture if requested, or simply be a quiet presence.

I've seen chaplains enter a room filled with milling and distressed family members and totally change the charged atmosphere. One emotionally exhausted, quietly sobbing husband refused to take a break from his wife's side. The chaplain pulled up a chair and sat beside him. After a while he asked, "How did you two meet?" That question led to an afternoon of reminiscing, laughter, and tears among family members, followed by a prayer service.

"Tell me about your work," I once urged Chaplain Matthew, an accomplished storyteller and southern gentleman. He happily obliged.

"I see a lot of reconciliation and healing at the hospice bedside. When I know that some unresolved issue exists, I call family members and tell them time is running out. I say, 'If you want to see your loved one alive, if there is anything you want to say, this is the time to come.' Often that little prod will set forgiveness and reconciliation in motion. I always offer to be there. Mostly I don't say much, just observe and marvel at the healing power of forgiveness. Aloud, or in my thoughts, I offer prayers of gratitude.

"People who take comfort in their faith usually have an easier death. For those who tell me they have been unfaithful to God or to others, I remind them that faith is a process. Just because we don't get it all right in this life doesn't mean that we won't be welcomed home.

"When I visited a Jewish woman, Deborah, in hospice care, she asked, 'Could you arrange for a rabbi to visit me?'

"I stopped by a few days later and she said, 'That rabbi was very nice, but could you find a woman rabbi?'

"When I saw her again, she said, 'That woman rabbi was really nice, but could you visit me instead?'"

What happened next was the rapid growth of an unlikely friendship and a remarkable spiritual journey shared by a Jewish mother and a southern preacher. Matthew, a biblical scholar, and Deborah, well schooled in the Torah, found common ground in the Old Testament and a God whose presence they both experienced. Their discussions were a mutual source of illumination and stimulation. "Deborah was the godliest woman I ever met. She lived her faith," Matthew said.

Deborah invited Matthew to officiate at her funeral. "Please, just don't bring up Jesus," she asked. At the memorial service, Matthew spoke in Hebrew to praise and honor Deborah. Her family were touched by his skillful tribute and comforting service.

When another chaplain, Denise, visited her patient Ella, she discovered the woman had just died. Immediately the chaplain called Sally, Ella's daughter.

"Please, please, don't leave my mother alone," Sally pleaded. "Stay with her; I'll be there in half an hour."

"I'll be here," Denise promised. A hospice nurse and Denise worked quickly to prepare Ella's body for her daughter's arrival. They bathed her, put in her false teeth, combed her hair, and changed her gown and sheets. As she dimmed the lights in the room, Denise noted that it had been 45 minutes since she had spoken to Sally, so she called again. In a slightly slurred voice, Sally assured her, "I'm on my way."

In the newly deceased, the body starts to stiffen within hours after death. Before rigor mortis set in, Denise and the nurse positioned Ella's body so that she appeared at peace. Noticing that her hands were becoming cold, they massaged them with lotion to keep them warm and pliable in the expectation that Sally would arrive momentarily.

Another 45 minutes passed. A hospital nurse stepped in the room and asked, "How soon may we remove her body, and which funeral home should we call?"

"I don't know. Give us a little more time," Denise pleaded. Still no Sally. Several phone calls and two hours later Sally arrived, disheveled, unsteady, and relieved to see Denise still waiting for her. "I'm really sorry," Sally began, explaining that she'd stopped for a few fortifying drinks on the way.

With no annoyance, no scolding, no judgment, Denise embraced Sally and moved with her to the bedside. At Sally's request they prayed together, and then the daughter asked to have a few minutes alone with her mother. As she left the room, Denise watched Sally gently lift and kiss her mother's hand.

Music Therapist. "Music takes away negativity," commented a seasoned music therapist. The power of music to calm human suffering—whether the patient is in physical, emotional, or spiritual pain—is remarkable. The first time I heard a music therapist at work, I stood in wonder as ethereal harp music floated through the halls. I watched the housekeepers gather in the doorway of a patient's room, mopping the same spot over and over as they listened, enchanted. Even patients with dementia who have not spoken for years sometimes respond to their favorite music by mouthing words or moving an arm in time to the beat of the melody.

Music transforms us, stimulates memories, and transports us to another time and place. Think back to the music that once moved you and the feelings that accompanied it. Recall a tune from long ago, and chances are you will remember some lyrics as well.

Family members often mirror their loved one's distress. Visiting Caroline, I found a group huddled over her restless body, all of them trying to soothe her, none of them succeeding. At the suggestion of the nurse, a music therapist visited the home and inquired about Caroline's music preferences. Almost always, an agitated patient will begin to relax in response to an old favorite.

The therapist sang songs from *South Pacific*, accompanying herself on the guitar. As Caroline's agitation eased, family members started to relax too. Before long, one son wandered into the living room to lie back in a recliner; another yawned deeply and walked off in search of a blanket, while the third simply headed for the guest bedroom, where the sound of his snoring soon competed with the music. After one such session, I reached for a patient's boom box, eager to put in a tape to continue the music. The music therapist stopped me and said, "No need. The brain continues to 'hear' the music for at least thirty minutes. Playing a tape now would interfere with the lasting benefits of the music already played."

Triage. The triage team works through the night to answer telephone calls from patients and family members. "No question is dumb or asked too often," one triage nurse explained. "We may not get a second chance to get it right." When appropriate, the triage staff will send team members to a patient's home to provide care and support.

Outreach and Education. The outreach team educates healthcare professionals and the lay community about hospice. The more information that goes out to the public, the more likely that patients and families will benefit from all that hospice has to offer.

Grief Counselors. Grief, a normal process before and after the death of a loved one, can be overwhelming. The hospice bereavement team is available to offer support to loved ones, both children and adults. Counselors can ease the suffering that may unexpectedly wash over a survivor.

An 86-year-old man, married for over 60 years, asked Carlos, his bereavement counselor, "How can I feel so sad and so relieved at the same time?" Carlos reassured him that his feelings were normal. "Your wife's death ended her suffering and your despair. Your sense of relief has nothing to do with how much you loved her."

"It takes whatever it takes," reflected Carlos. "Grief is as individual as each person, reflected Carlos."

Office Staff. "Hospice Central" is made up of extraordinary office staff members who support the field staff, welcome calls from patients and family members, and sustain the hospice infrastructure on a daily basis.

Volunteers. Hospice volunteers range in age from teenagers to seniors and provide a variety of services including administrative work and support for patients and family members. (For an in-depth discussion of the volunteer's role, see the section titled "The Calling" in the Prequel.)

Possessed of a "whatever it takes" attitude, the hospice team collaborates to bring a powerful presence to the hospice bedside.

FURTHER CONSIDERATIONS ON THE HOSPICE TEAM

If you had a bad skin rash, you'd seek a dermatologist. Severe headaches? Look for a neurologist. A terminal illness? Contact hospice, the experts in end-of-life care. No one does it better. Hospice can make the unbearable seem bearable and bring hope to what seems like a hopeless situation.

Contact your local hospice for a free consultation and for more information about the services hospice offers, advance directives, Do Not Resuscitate orders, feeding tubes and artificial food and fluid, comfort measures, the use of antibiotics at the end of life, ventilators, and pain and symptom management.

CHAPTER 7

Managing Pain and Uncomfortable Symptoms

WHEN I FIRST ASKED MY MOTHER TO TELL ME what it was like to be a student nurse over half a century ago, she chose to start by talking about pain. She reminded me that until about the middle of the twentieth century, most people died at home. Only gradually did death and dying move to hospitals, where in a shrunken world composed of an iron bed, a tiny bedside table, and a moveable green privacy curtain, poorly medicated, suffering people waited to die. When she was in nursing school, she said, the medical profession was still emerging from the dark ages of pain control. Morphine was available, but its use was highly restricted. She explained:

> As a student nurse in a large city hospital, I took care of many dying people, most of them in pain. Early in training, students were initiated into a conspiracy of silence: "Never, ever tell a patient he was dying. Never admit that a patient had cancer. Refer all such inquiries to the doctor." However, the physicians, themselves overworked interns, were no better prepared than the nurses to ease the suffering of dying patients. Nurses knew that to call an exhausted intern snatching a few hours of sleep to come and talk to a patient about death was to risk hearing a

roar similar to the response they'd get from poking a sleeping grizzly bear with a sharp stick.

The rationale underlying such secrecy was simple but incredibly flawed: tell someone that they were dying and the shock of the news might kill them! Despite a patient's obvious suffering, we were taught to suspect that they might be faking it to get more morphine, the only really effective painkiller we had. Therefore, to prevent addiction, regardless of the degree of suffering, most patients were held to the same strict standard: one morphine injection every four hours.

"Breakthrough pain" was a phrase not yet coined to name the pain that surfaces between scheduled doses of pain medications. For those who begged for more frequent relief, we administered a placebo, an injection of sterile saline, while maintaining the fiction that we were injecting morphine. If someone complained too loudly, we might be told to wheel the patient's bed to a room at the end of a long corridor and close the door until it was time for the next morphine shot. Without such a heartless regimen, we were told, patients would surely become addicted. Why addiction was even a concern for a dying person still baffles me.

My mother described desperate patients who were discovered to have saved and hidden their bedtime sleeping pills for an escape to suicide if pain became unbearable. When a student discovered a stockpile under a mattress, she was to confiscate the pills and turn them over to the head nurse.

"Looking back, it seems like torture but no one knew any better." She recalled one of her favorite patients:

Because most of our terminally ill patients stayed in the hospital to die, many would lie in residence for months. Students came to know patients well, and we often formed a close emotional tie. My favorite was Carl, a sweet, childless widower. Each morning as I made his bed, he told me stories of his life as a merchant seaman in World War II. On a rust-bucket ship, dodging Nazi submarines, he helped deliver food and munitions to England.

Reading Carl's chart, I learned that although he'd recently survived extensive surgery for colon cancer, no one had told him he had cancer or that the disease had already spread to nearby organs.

Things changed rapidly after his surgery. Each day, Carl became more gaunt as he lost weight and acquired the yellowish skin so typical of such wraiths. Although he suffered constant pain, he rarely complained and waited patiently for his shot of morphine. Then one day he asked me to pull the curtain around his bed. "I'm not getting better," he whispered. "Tell me the truth. Do I have cancer?" In those days cancer almost always meant a certain death sentence.

I knew this good man liked me, trusted me, and hoped I might be the one person who would tell him the truth. Nevertheless, as I avoided looking into his sunken eyes, I parroted what I was taught to say: "I don't know. You'll have to talk to your doctor about that." At that moment I believe his long-suffering spirit shattered.

I still recall the shame I felt when I lied to him. But I was a tiny speck in a dust storm of denial. If I broke the rules, I risked getting kicked out of nursing school. Moreover, I was totally ignorant as to what I might say to offer him comfort. As a result, he withdrew from me and listlessly turned away when I visited. He died in pain, lonely, hopeless, without human comfort.

Not until the 1960s, when Dame Cicely Saunders smashed the old rules with one sharp bang of her hospice hammer, did things really begin to change. Setting the model for the rest of the world, she founded the modern hospice movement. Her dying patients received Brompton cocktails, concoctions containing liquid morphine, given as often and as generously as needed. Emotional, spiritual, and medical needs were addressed with loving attention.

Despite continuing advances in pain and symptom management, many Americans still die in pain. Patients in hospitals often report moderate to severe pain before dying, while patients receiving hospice care typically report excellent pain and symptom management. Hospice professionals, widely acknowledged as pain management experts, operate with a philosophy that all pain and other uncomfortable symptoms are treatable and everyone is entitled to relief. Nothing is gained by gritting teeth and suffering silently.

Hospice trusts patients as accurate judges of their own discomfort. In assessing its severity, a hospice professional is likely to ask, "On a scale of zero to ten with ten as the worst pain you've ever had and zero meaning no pain, how do you rate your discomfort?" Then the hospice team works together to address all the patient's needs by gathering detailed information about pain and other symptoms, a history of the disease, current medications, family dynamics, and emotional and spiritual needs.

"What does 'quality of life' mean to you?" a team member may ask before coming up with a treatment plan to meet a patient's individual needs. One patient may ask for more medication to ease severe pain, while another willingly tolerates more discomfort for the trade-off of being more alert. In extreme cases, a patient or family may request heavy sedation (called palliative or terminal sedation), sometimes to the point of unconsciousness, to escape intractable suffering.

A patient's wife once cornered me to ask, "Doesn't hospice really kill people?" Her naked question is not usually expressed so openly, but it lurks in the minds of many. Of course people die while receiving hospice care; however, they die from their disease process, not from hospice care. Hospice care honors a natural dying process while aggressively managing pain and other uncomfortable symptoms.

"Don't use a sledgehammer to kill a flea," advise hospice experts. Wherever possible, hospice starts treatment with small amounts of nonnarcotic, over-the-counter drugs, like acetaminophen or ibuprofen. If that works, fine. If not, then the hospice team will go up the pain relief ladder until they get the desired relief as defined by the patient and caregivers. As a disease progresses, sometimes pain will spike, necessitating an adjustment in medications.

Not every dying person suffers pain. Not one of my four grandparents died in physical discomfort. Linda was not so fortunate. Early in my career, I visited her home with a hospice nurse to assist with the admission process. Linda's breast cancer had spread to her bones, and she was in severe pain.

Linda's husband Burt was a retired physician who had practiced medicine for over 40 years. Now his full-time job was taking care of his wife. Worried and frustrated, Burt told me, "My wife is no wimp. We've managed all right until recently, but now she's crying, complaining of unbearable pain, even as I keep increasing her morphine! She's getting enough to kill a horse but with no relief. What's going on?"

The hospice nurse explained, "Relief from bone pain requires an over-the-counter nonsteroidal, anti-inflammatory drug (NSAID) like ibuprofen." Given ibuprofen, Linda had significant pain relief within 24 hours. Burt admitted that he had believed the morphine alone would kill any pain. "Pain management was never my specialty," he acknowledged humbly.

Family members often question hospice's use of opioids like morphine. "Won't my loved one become an addict?" they ask. When opioids are used appropriately for pain relief, patients do not become addicts. On the contrary, they gain relief from agonizing distress. Unlike those addicted to drugs, a hospice patient whose pain is under control will usually not request more medication. Nevertheless, tolerance for larger doses of opioids can increase as a disease progresses and pain intensifies. In such cases the hospice team, led by the physician, will adjust doses, switch medications, or try different combinations of potent painkillers until comfort is achieved.

Sometimes patients who are taking opioids improve enough that they no longer need such powerful drugs. Then the team will carefully manage weaning the patient to avoid unpleasant side effects.

My mother told me of an elderly lady who once grabbed her hand and pleaded, "Please, please put a pillow over my head. I want to die!" It's not unusual for someone tortured by unrelieved suffering to beg to die. However, with hospice care, not only can pain be effectively managed, but other uncomfortable symptoms like nausea, vomiting, restlessness, agitation, and difficulty breathing can be brought under control. When such ailments are managed well, the will to live typically returns.

Many people ask about the difference between hospice care and palliative care. Palliative care is intended to ease any type of pain and suffering and is available at any time during a patient's illness. It can be delivered along with life-prolonging and curative treatments. Not all palliative care is hospice care, but all hospice care is palliative because hospice seeks to bring the dying patient relief from pain and other discomforts. Many hospice programs offer palliative care as a separate service for patients who may need pain and symptom management, although they are not ready for hospice care. To learn more about palliative care, see Appendix E.

FURTHER CONSIDERATIONS ON PAIN

Pain is considered the fifth vital sign. Most healthcare workers are required to check for pain, just as they do for temperature, blood pressure, pulse, and respiratory rate. A hospice nurse recalled a big, burly retired army officer. When she asked him whether he was in pain, he grimaced and said no. She replied, "I don't want you to be brave; I want you to be comfortable."

One of the biggest fears for all of us is, *Will it hurt when I die?* Dying does not have to hurt. The choice is yours.

PART THREE

THE DYING TIME

CHAPTER 8

Attitudes and Choices

PEOPLE APPROACH THE LOSS OF A LIFE IN DIFFERENT WAYS. Many never consider that they can choose an attitude toward dying. For patients and caregivers alike, deciding on an attitude to deal with difficult times can actually ease the suffering that so often surrounds the dying process.

Elderly people who have been ill for a long time and have no hope for recovery may be accepting and even eager to hasten the dying process. After enduring several strokes and a heart attack, a weary man said to his wife, "Dying is easy; it's living that's hard."

Some patients demonstrate such a determined attitude and such a mighty will to live that they almost convince others they will escape death. Actually, some do. In spite of all predictions to the contrary, even after facing a terminal diagnosis, they live on, at least for a while. Ray was not one of them.

At 54, strikingly handsome, with dark wavy hair and a tinge of gray at the temples, Ray was successful in all the ways the world admires. A powerful, self-made multimillionaire, he had a beautiful wife, two married daughters, and a grandchild on the way. Ray owned vintage cars, boats, a local mansion, and vacation homes in warm climates. He took pride in his benevolent control of a small empire; he established a model profit-sharing plan with employees; he gave generously to his church and community. However, a ruthless, fast-moving killer—pancreatic cancer—proved an invincible enemy.

I met Ray after he'd traveled the world in efforts to tame his beast or at least slow its relentless takeover of his body. Reluctant to enter hospice care because it represented failure to him, at the urging of his physician he finally agreed to hospice for pain and symptom management and for the support available to his distraught family.

With hospice care, Ray's physical pain was quickly brought under control. Spiritually, he was at peace; he spoke of his strong faith and the certainty that his deceased mother and brother were waiting for him. However, Ray suffered inconsolable grief over having to leave his family.

Ray had a rage to live. He and other fighters like him do not give up easily. Familiar with power, they hate to relinquish control or lose any battle. No matter the odds, even when there is no cure, until the last moment they struggle to beat back death.

Ray explained, "I would give away everything I own just to spend one more day with my family. They love me; they depend on me; I see how devastated they are, and I can't do anything to help them."

"No one ever died wishing they had spent more time at the office" goes an old saying. The closer people move toward death, the more they seem to realize what is most important in life. You can't work in hospice for very long before learning that loving relationships are the glue that binds people together after everything else—titles, careers, awards, and material possessions—melts away. In the end, the only wealth that mattered to Ray was his family.

Even as his body gave out, his ferocious spirit fought on. When he was encouraged to relax, he protested, "Don't you understand? If I relax, I'll go to sleep. If I go to sleep, I won't wake up." Ray was right. When he finally closed his eyes out of exhaustion, he died almost instantly. Acceptance was never a choice for him.

If Ray was at one end of the attitude continuum, Morrie Schwartz was at the other. In *Tuesdays with Morrie*, Mitch Albom wrote about his beloved college professor who was dying of amyotrophic lateral sclerosis. ALS is a wasting neurological disease with no cure.

Morrie too grieved the fading away of his well-loved life, but he did so with an attitude of graceful acceptance that inspired admiration throughout the world. Morrie believed that true liberation is letting go of everything. Instead of fighting like Ray, Morrie took pleasure in spending his remaining moments with friends and family. Always the professor, sharing his bountiful wisdom, he reminded others that they are more than flesh and bones. He taught that death is not terrible but the next phase of an eternal journey.

Not everyone clings to life with Ray's tenacity or faces the end of life with the grace of Morrie Schwartz. Ultimately, the meaning one gives to any life circumstance determines one's response. Everything can be taken from a person but one thing, and that is "to choose one's attitude in any given set of circumstances." In these words, Nazi concentration camp survivor Viktor Frankl wrote of his suffering in *Man's Search for Meaning* and thereby offered hope to countless others who feel helpless in the vise of escalating events.

"Don't be afraid to endure some emotional suffering," advised a hospice social worker. "Seeking to escape all suffering can interrupt or delay the process. Sometimes experiencing the darkness for a while allows us to move to a deeper place." Those who are willing to acknowledge and experience their suffering, and talk about it with a trusted friend or counselor, may come to a better understanding of the meaning of their trials. Without seeking to avoid the process, they may achieve tremendous personal growth, compassion for themselves and others, and a new understanding of their purpose in life.

FURTHER CONSIDERATIONS ON HOPE

For patients and loved ones who choose a hopeful attitude, the wisdom of a hospice nurse may be useful. "Hope is the last thing to go," she said. "Almost everyone hopes for a long and healthy life. When we learn that we have a life-threatening illness, we hope that the diagnosis is wrong, or that we will recover, or that the illness will go into remission. If a condition worsens, we are likely to hope to live as long as possible. Given only a short time to live, we hope to spend quality time with those we love. When only days remain, we hope to stay free of pain and anxiety and to find the words to express affection and gratitude to loved ones. When only hours remain, we hope that death will be peaceful. Hope reaches even beyond death; most of us hope that family and friends will remember us and that we will be together again."

CHAPTER 9

What's It Like to Die?

"D IVINA, WHAT'S IT LIKE TO DIE?" asked Jolene, a middle-aged wife and mother whose aggressive breast cancer had shot tentacles throughout her body. For months, Divina had been Jolene's hospice nurse. On this morning, with her mind clear and pain under control, Jolene opened a *conversation* she had obviously considered for some time. It is not unusual for a hospice professional to function as a trusted confidant who can listen to a patient's deepest fears without flinching.

Aware that Jolene's death was near, Divina knew her patient needed more information and was ready to hear it. She moved close to the bedside, sat down, and took Jolene's hand.

"Well," she began, "the death rate is one hundred percent. Dying is as natural as being born. Every life ends in death.

"What I can tell you is that those who are close to dying and have their physical, emotional, and spiritual needs met often radiate an aura of acceptance and surrender. If they could speak, I think they would say something like this: 'I'm through fighting. I know I am about to die and I'm ready. I'm at peace.'"

"But how do you get to that point?" Jolene persisted.

Divina knew that Jolene would not accept evasive responses or empty reassurances, and that anything she said would carry a powerful message that could either instill calm and courage or stir fear and anxiety. She chose her words carefully.

"Jolene, you've had chemotherapy, radiation, surgery, alternative treatments, and the support and prayers of many loving people. These things bought you more time. For everyone, however, there comes a point when nothing more can be done to stop the process of dying.

"I think many things come together to make for a good death. Acceptance of your circumstances is one key. I once heard someone compare dying to being a trapeze artist. The trick is for the flyer to relax and let the catcher do the work of bringing her over to safety.

"Faith gives a powerful boost to acceptance. The belief that something good lies beyond this life offers hope and peace of mind that make dying easier. Many people report being greeted by deceased loved ones shortly before they die. When I ask patients, 'Have you seen your mother yet?' a common response is 'How did you know?'

"You have the loving support of your family. You've raised wonderful children and you've talked often with your husband about how to go on without you. You know that your family cherishes you, that you'll be missed, and that you will live on in their hearts. We are all prepared to take care of you through the last moment so you will die peacefully in your own bed.

"Your pain is under control now, and you will not suffer at the end. You will receive medication as often as necessary. Your family members know what to do, and the hospice team is always a phone call away, day or night."

Jolene was silent. Thoughtful.

Divina continued. "This much I know, Jolene. When a soul transitions from this earth free of pain, peaceful, supported by loved ones, cared for by hospice, there are no words to adequately describe the wonder of it. I promise you, you will die well. I've never had a patient die in pain, and you're not going to be the first!"

Not long after that conversation, Jolene began a rapid downhill slide. Everyone expected her to die quickly; however, she seemed to hover with one foot in this world and the other foot already in the next. Sometimes people linger for days, even weeks, before they finally let go. One morning Jolene was barely responsive. Her decline inched forward until she was only breathing five times a minute. (Normal breaths occur about 16 to 20 times a minute.) No one expected that she could last through the day.

Knowing that many patients prefer to die alone, Divina urged Jolene's exhausted family members to take a walk in the early spring sunshine. When they returned, Jolene had stopped breathing. Her daughter told me later, "Thinking Mom had died, we all leaned over her at the same time, watching to see if she'd take another breath. Forty-five seconds later she gasped her last breath, one that seemed to come up forcefully, from the bottom of her lungs. We all jumped back in surprise. Slaphappy from the ups and downs of our long vigil, we started laughing. Given Mom's sense of humor, we agreed that she was laughing with us." As Divina promised, Jolene died peacefully.

Just as everyone lives their own life, everyone dies their own death. "People tend to die as they lived" goes an old saying. Death may enter with the quiet elegance of a ballerina or barge in with the crushing, repetitive punches of a prizefighter. For some, dying seems a massive struggle, while others pass quietly and quickly. Others, like Jolene, plateau for a while, then decline slowly. People with dementia often depart over many years, progressively losing mental and physical capabilities until it seems that nothing is left of the person once known.

Because so many people today live past middle age without witnessing a dying process or being present at a death, some basic information about what happens follows. Although the dying process is unique for each individual, there are predictable signs that the end is near. Not everyone experiences all the signs described below. They are included here to help you understand that what you see during the dying time is normal. Except for controlling pain and other uncomfortable symptoms, there is no need for aggressive treatments.

Withdrawal. Dying people often show a diminished desire to visit or talk and lack of interest in what goes on around them. More dozing and longer periods of sleep further indicate that a person is preparing to die. Loved ones may feel hurt or excluded, hoping perhaps for touching words of gratitude or a final declaration of love. Such behavior is not rejection but simply part of withdrawing from this world. Hearing is the first sense acquired in the womb and the last sense to go, so even those who appear to have lost consciousness can often sense the presence of others. Identify yourself, gently touch, hold a hand, speak in a normal tone of voice, and offer comforting reassurance: "I'm here for you."

Decreased Food and Fluid Intake. Patients do not die because they stop eating, they stop eating because they are dying. Family members often fuss and fret about what to feed or not to feed a dying person, coaxing them to eat, worrying if they don't. "If we can just convince him to eat, surely he will get better," goes the reasoning, because all through life we look to food to sustain and nurture and help us recover from illness.

When the body's message seems to be "No more," follow the patient's lead. Hospice doesn't encourage dying people to eat food they don't want; a diminishing appetite is far more common than not. When it comes to food and drink at the end of life, less is more. A good motto is "Offer, but don't force."

I've seen elaborate, beautifully presented full-course meals go untouched except perhaps for an obligatory bite to please the gift bearer. Knowing it was his father's favorite food, one man proudly presented him with a broiled lobster tail dripping with butter. Disappointed when the old man pushed it away, his son protested, "But Dad, lobster is your favorite food!"

What this caring son didn't understand was that food that once seemed delectable can become offensive to a dying person. Cooking odors, cigarette smoke lingering on clothing, perfumed lotions, even the scent of flowers may be irritating as well. Make the sickroom a fragrance-free zone to avoid introducing unnecessary discomfort.

The desire for food and liquids fades markedly at the end of life. Loss of appetite is a natural sign that the body is preparing to shut down. The resulting dehydration triggers the release of endorphins in the body, which aid in natural pain relief. Dehydration also prevents the uncomfortable accumulation of excess fluid in body tissues.

Forcing food and fluids gets in the way of a natural and comfortable dying process for someone who is terminally ill. The medical evidence is clear: dehydration at the end of life aids a natural and compassionate death. It is medically, legally, and ethically appropriate to withhold or discontinue food and fluids that are no longer beneficial.

Family members can offer sips of juice, water, or ice chips, keep the mouth moist with glycerin swabs, and use lip balm to prevent lips from cracking. If a loved one wants sips of liquids and is having difficulty swallowing, elevate the head of the bed, use a small spoon, and proceed slowly. It may take a long time to swallow a few sips, so use these opportunities to offer comforting words and a caring presence.

Circulation. Circulation decreases at the end of life because the heart can no longer pump blood efficiently throughout the body. As a result, nail beds may turn bluish, skin can take on a mottled look resembling bruising, and extremities may feel increasingly cool to the touch. When hands and feet feel cold, light nonelectric blankets may help. Also, flushing, fever, and sweating may come and go as the body loses the ability to regulate body temperature.

Changes in Breathing. Breathing may become shallow, irregular, and more labored. Breaths often slow down, or they may speed up with long lapses in between. The sound of air moving over mucus in the upper airway is called the "death rattle." Although unsettling for family members, it seems to cause no discomfort for patients. Deep suctioning is not advisable because it does cause discomfort and can actually increase secretions. All these changes can be frightening, although each is part of the normal dying process. Medications are available to dry up mucus and ease breathing. Hospice also teaches simple skills such as changing position to make it easier to breathe.

Incontinence and Decrease in Urine Output. Urine typically darkens in color and decreases in volume as dehydration progresses and the kidneys shut down. Bowel and bladder incontinence may occur. Not everyone loses control, but it is wise to keep a supply of adult diapers and absorbent pads to prevent major accidents and avoid frequent bed changes. Hospice teaches family members how to lift, move, and turn patients to keep them clean and comfortable.

Restlessness and Agitation. "Jerome wanted to be up, sit in a chair, then get back in bed, all within five minutes," reported his weary wife. "Fifteen minutes later he wanted to do it all over again." Restlessness and agitation (sometimes called terminal agitation) are common in the dying time. People may pick at the sheets and pull at their bed clothing. Body chemistry changes and decreased oxygen to the brain can cause distressing behaviors. Sometimes such symptoms indicate an unresolved issue or unfinished business. People who are close to death often speak of travel. They may mention a train, airplane, bus, or car or try to get dressed to "go out," "get in line," or "buy tickets." Many patients will say they "want to go home." These behaviors are often a clue that death is near.

Hospice can be helpful in identifying causes of behaviors and supplying remedies. Once again, emotional and spiritual support and calming medications are readily available to reduce anxiety and ease discomfort.

Personality Changes. Liza is a longtime hospice home health aide. She put her life on hold to move back home and help care for her dying father. After several months, Liza's mother encouraged her to accept an invitation to meet friends for dinner. When she said good-bye to her dad for the evening, he responded harshly, "Go ahead and go. You don't do anything around here anyway." Liza was devastated. "I knew that mean comment was the disease talking, not my dad, but it still hurt."

Sometimes very ill people seem resentful, ungrateful, and dissatisfied with everyone and everything: noise is unbearable; caregiver efforts to move or change them are intolerable; favorite foods are nauseating. In such instances, caregivers can feel unappreciated and overworked. However, responses like "I'll be more careful" or "I'm sorry I hurt you" can help avoid a defensive, argumentative reaction and reinforce a loved one's chosen attitude of patience and perseverance.

Sensory Experiences. A dying person may look past you to focus on an unseen presence. Or they may wave their arms or smile and seem to reach out to someone you cannot see. Whatever is reported or not reported, seen or not seen, the most comforting thing you can do is simply accept such behavior without interfering. Whatever dying people report is real to them.

Death. Shortly before death occurs, in lighter-skinned people you may observe the skin turn a yellowish color. You will know that death has occurred when a person does not respond, is not breathing, and does not have a pulse or a heartbeat. Eyelids may open; pupils become fixed and blinking ceases. The jaw may relax and the mouth open. A final loss of bowel and bladder control may occur.

Hospice services continue after death, helping with whatever is needed. Even though a hospice patient dies, his or her loved ones may still need emotional support or assistance in coping with the many details that accompany a death.

It sometimes happens that the signs of dying described above are prolonged or so distressing that family members panic and call 911. But what happens next may not be in the patient's best interests or consistent with their wishes. An ambulance will take the patient to a hospital emergency room, where the person will usually die or be placed on life support. Very few of these patients survive. One 30-year veteran hospital nurse, part of her hospital emergency response team, told me that she responds to an average of two "code blues" a day, most of them for the frail elderly or terminally ill. "In all that time, I have yet to see a single person survive long enough to leave the hospital," she said. "If more people had timely conversations about DNRs, this wouldn't happen," she added.

Stuck in her grief almost a year after her husband's death, Rachel sobbed as she said, "We married late in life. Neither of us had children or close relatives, so to find each other brought us great joy. In fact, we'd never been happier in our entire lives. When Michael was diagnosed with advanced lymphoma and told that he had only a short time to live, he said that he wanted to die at home. Back then I didn't know about hospice.

"We had some good days, and I felt strong enough to manage without help until we came close to the end and I couldn't make him comfortable. He was moaning and gasping for air. I panicked! I could not bear the sights or the sounds of my Michael's suffering. Despite all our careful plans to have him die at home, I lost my nerve and called 911. Paramedics performed CPR, shocked his heart, and rushed him to the hospital, where he was intubated. He died in the emergency room, only minutes before I could get there. I failed him."

Alone, with no preparation for the frightening changes in Michael's appearance and behavior, Rachel felt overwhelmed and unable to fulfill her promise. She sought bereavement counseling for complicated grief and came to accept that she did the best she could do at the time. She no longer blames herself for what happened and has progressed in mourning her loss.

When an approaching death is prepared for and hospice services are utilized, when family members know what to expect and how to respond, panic usually gives way to a tranquil death. An expected death is never an emergency.

FURTHER CONSIDERATIONS ON OFFERING HELP

When families are in crisis, expressions of caring and support are appreciated. Rather than ask, "Is there anything I can do?" do something. Mail a card, write a personal note, deliver a meal, run errands, walk the dog, clean the house, provide respite care, or take care of children. Even if help is not accepted, your thoughtfulness will make a difference.

CHAPTER 10

Listen

"**A**MY, HONEY, BUY ME A POWERBALL TICKET," directed Nana, a 92-year-old great-grandmother, as she shuffled along in her voluminous flowered muumuu and bedroom slippers worn flat at the heels. "Then pick up two double espresso lattes and a couple of bran muffins," she continued as she handed her 30-year-old granddaughter a handful of dollars.

When Amy returned carrying a coffeehouse bag and waving what she laughingly declared would be Nana's winning ticket, she announced, "When the cashier asked me if I wanted the payout in one lump sum or twenty payments over twenty years, I choose the twenty payments option."

"Honey, what were you thinking? I'm ninety-two!" Nana sputtered. "I have emphysema, two bad hips, and sky-high blood pressure. Not to mention hemorrhoids and arthritis." Amy's eyes widened, then welled with tears. "But Nana, I never thought you would *die!*"

In the past, when Nana spoke of her failing health, Amy tuned her out. Of course she knew her beloved Nana would die someday, but because "someday" was not *now*, she simply refused to think about it. Amy's denial is a self-protective defense that comes in all sizes and at all ages to protect a person temporarily from a painful truth.

Nana took no offense at Amy's behavior because she was still fully engaged in life and determined not to die until she won the lottery.

Contrast Nana's story to that of Dee, a contemporary, who wanted to die and needed her family to understand her misery and really listen.

Wrapped in a fuzzy pink shawl, and sunk into the confines of her recliner, Dee at 92 was mentally alert but physically a wreck. "I've out-lived my life and I'm ready to go," she told her family. Dee had already fought a good battle. Twenty years earlier she had survived a near-fatal accident and lengthy recovery. Back then, she had welcomed the family "fight" chants that boosted her will to live and put her in the fast lane to recovery.

"She's a fighter!" declared Dee's devoted sons, Don and Dean, as they proudly described her lifelong traits of stubbornness and independence. So when their mother calmly announced that she would no longer take her medications and that she had canceled all future medical appointments, they objected loudly: "You can't do that! It's not time to give up, Mom!"

Adult children who observe an elderly parent's decline often react like Dee's sons, who responded in the only way they knew how: with loud protests, scolding, and increased pressure to keep fighting. Dee was not resisting her sons for the sake of her independence. She was long past that. She knew that her best efforts could not improve the quality of her life or fix what ailed her. Dee chose to forgo medical interventions that she considered useless, risky, costly, and likely to increase her dependence and prolong her decline.

"I just want them to listen to me. Those boys—ages sixty-four and sixty-eight—leave me feeling guilty, as though I've let them down. Why can't they accept that I can't fight anymore and that I'll welcome death?"

A feeling is neither right nor wrong. It just is. To be told, "You shouldn't feel that way," is rarely helpful advice for anyone. "I know how you feel" may be the second-least-helpful counsel. Dee's sons laid claim to feelings they had yet to experience. A neutral acknowledgment like, "This must be hard for you," or "Help us understand what you are feeling," and then remaining silent while listening to their mother's response, might have been more beneficial.

Fortunately, listening is a skill that can be learned. The most meaningful *conversations* take place when people are fully present, without distraction and with a generous intent to listen and accept what is heard. When you turn off the TV, mute the telephone, and sit down at eye level next to someone (as opposed to standing in the doorway), you convey caring. Moreover, visits to the bedside can offer caregivers an oasis, a few moments to relax.

Indicate your willingness to listen by inquiring, "What's on your mind?" or "How is your spirit today?" or "What do you understand about how things are going?" Such questions can provide an opening, an invitation to confide fears and worries that might otherwise be held back so as not to offend or alienate someone on whom a patient depends.

"God gave us two ears and one mouth for a reason," goes an old saying. Its message is that we should listen twice as much as we talk. If you wait at least seven seconds after someone stops speaking, chances are good that they'll continue talking, perhaps revealing something they've been hesitant to say.

Try not to finish other people's sentences unless you are certain they cannot finish without your help. Withhold advice unless asked. Good listeners often repeat back the last word or two of what was said or say, "Tell me more" and "What do you mean?" to continue a conversation.

A gentle word of caution: It is hard to imagine the total, bottom-of-the-glass exhaustion that many dying people feel as life ebbs away. The effort to turn in bed, or even lift a hand can seem impossible. Common signs of such total fatigue include closed eyes, deep sighs, and a failure to answer a question or cooperate with a request. Rather than urge a response, consider asking, "Would you like to rest now?" or "Shall we talk more later?" and accepting a brief nod yes or no as an answer.

Warm friendships and intimate conversations often develop between hospice workers and patients, who may speak more freely to a virtual stranger than to a family member, as was the case with Ira and Vincent.

Vincent, a hospice patient, was clearly approaching the end of his days. When Ira, a seasoned hospice volunteer, arrived at Vincent's home, he was met at the door by Emma, Vincent's niece. She said, "He's not going to talk to you; he doesn't talk to anyone. We think he's deaf."

"Well, then, I'll just sit with him," replied Ira.

The silent Vincent, a tiny man with a bald, freckled scalp, looked like a bump beneath his blanket. Ira noticed near the bed a faded photo of a skinny young soldier from World War II.

"That you?" he asked. Vincent nodded and his eyes brightened with interest. Ira gently closed the door.

"I landed at Omaha Beach. Second day. Second Division, Infantry. Came in on a landing craft. Nearly drowned before I reached the beach," Ira offered. "What about you?"

"Third Army. Saw heavy action. Then we marched into Paris. Oh, those French girls!" replied the suddenly talkative Vincent.

Over the following weeks, the old warriors kept up a lively exchange as they refought long-ago battles. Each time Vincent pulled out another dusty recollection, Ira asked, "And then what happened?" Ira listened as Vincent unlocked his memories and reviewed his life. And when Vincent could no longer respond, Ira returned on schedule to sit with his friend.

Life review is a normal, healthy, and often necessary process for those who sense their life is nearing an end and want their story to be told.

The stories people tell often help them achieve understanding, accept the good and bad, resolve conflicts, and experience healing. A receptive and nonjudgmental listener can facilitate a life review and help a person to make sense of it all.

"How are you doing?" Every day millions of people ask that question to millions of other people who respond "Fine," even though both may be suffering greatly. The ending of a life can offer precious opportunities for authentic connections between people who care deeply for each other but may withhold their feelings to maintain a façade of strength and protect a loved one from overwhelming emotions. The admission of fears and anxieties does not indicate weakness. Listening to one another exchange honest expressions of sadness and loss as well as words of love can be both gratifying and consoling.

Even if you're in the habit of talking over others, mentally composing a list of sharp retorts, or impatiently waiting for your turn to speak, it's not too late to learn to listen. Now is always a good moment to begin.

FURTHER CONSIDERATIONS ON LIFE REVIEW

Many people find satisfaction and meaning in telling their life story. The following prompts may help facilitate a life review process.

- *Tell me about your childhood.*
- *Tell me about your family.*
- *How did you meet your spouse/partner?*
- *When you were young, what did you want to become?*
- *What kind of work have you done?*
- *Describe the happiest time in your life.*
- *Describe the saddest time in your life.*

- *What were your greatest challenges?*

- *What are you most proud of?*

- *What would you have done differently?*

- *How would you like to be remembered?*

The Hospice Foundation of America publishes a guide for conducting a life review. A Guide to Recalling and Telling Your Life Story is available at www.hospicefoundation.org. The Hospice Institute of the Florida Suncoast offers a toolkit, entitled Lifetime Legacies: A Life Review Toolkit, to teach life review to hospice staff and volunteers. See www.thehospice.org.

CHAPTER 11

Doctors Are Human, Too

D R. LUCIE AND I STOOD AT THE BEDSIDE of her father. Four months previously he had suffered a massive stroke that paralyzed his right side, requiring a ventilator to help him breathe and a feeding tube to provide nourishment. In the past few days his condition had worsened.

"Dad, can you hear me?" came Dr. Lucie's plea. Wringing her hands, she turned to me. "I'd give anything to have an urgent, blunt, and honest conversation with my father. I'm desperate to reach him and say, 'You've always guided me, given me good advice. Don't leave me here in the dark. Tell me, what do you want me to do now?'"

It was painful to watch her. Although she was an experienced physician, this day she was simply a daughter struggling with the decision of whether to admit her father to hospice care, remove the ventilator, and let him die a natural death.

We waited. Every few minutes she shouted into her father's ear: "Dad, this is Lucie. Do you want to stay on the vent?" Apparently he heard something, for he wiggled his Groucho Marx eyebrows at the sound of his daughter's voice. Louder this time: "Do... you... want... the ... ventilator... removed? Yes or no? Squeeze my hand once if it's yes and twice if it's no." He squeezed her hand four times. "Dad, was that four yeses or two nos?" She looked at me, hoping I would appreciate her sad attempt at humor.

Then, on the verge of tears, she said, "My father can't speak; he can't move or feed himself. He can't even scratch himself. My medical colleagues agree that he has no reasonable hope for recovery. What should I do?"

In the past I had observed Dr. Lucie in action and noted her decisive manner. Yet when we began to discuss the possibility of starting hospice care for her father, she appeared diminished in stature and shaken in confidence. She sat, shoulders slumped, hands tucked tightly between her knees, staring at the floor. She seemed more like a little girl than a highly skilled physician.

The immediate problem was that her father had failed to complete an advance directive, and neither he nor she had ever begun a conversation about how he would want to be treated if he became ill and unable to state his wishes.

Dr. Lucie seemed to be talking to herself as she began a remarkable confession. "I guess this is payback time for me." She sighed. "I've given false hope to my patients and their families when they needed to know the truth. Even when it was clearly time to bring in hospice, I'd often recommend one more aggressive treatment. I wanted to be the savior, fix everything." She went on, "It's difficult for physicians to discontinue treatments, even when we know they won't help, because it feels like failure."

Doctors are human beings who often carry a larger-than-life aura. Like everyone else, however, at times their judgment may be faulty. Doctors often overestimate the length of time their patients have to live, thereby depriving them of the benefits of hospice services. Many doctors balk at calling in hospice, even though there is no way they could provide all the services hospice offers. Reluctant doctors may be unwilling to stop curative treatments for a long-term patient, they may not fully understand hospice benefits, or they may mistakenly fear the financial consequences of losing Medicare payments when referring patients to hospice. That's why a second opinion and a free hospice consultation can make a big difference in the quality of life for a terminally ill patient.

Dr. Lucie and I talked for a long time that day. In the end, she signed the hospice consent forms for her father and authorized removal of his ventilator. The hospice nurse arrived within the hour. She examined Dr. Lucie's father and made preparations to remove the ventilator the next day. When the nurse returned the following morning, she carefully explained each step she took. Dr. Lucie looked on in surprise as her father watched the nurse's every move and gave her a weak thumbs-up. Almost immediately his hand started moving in small quick circles.

"You want to write something, Dad?" his daughter asked. Those eyebrows wiggled again. She put a pen in his hand and held a pad for him. After several illegible scrawls, Dr. Lucie read aloud, "He's writing, 'See Betty soon!' Betty is my mother; she died four years ago. He knows what is going on! He wants to let go. He   that it is his time and he will see my mother again!" Dr. Lucie wept as the nurse gently removed the ventilator.

Dr. Lucie expected her father to die immediately, but within minutes he was calmer, breathing easily, and a faint pink flush returned to his cheeks. The nurse moved him to a chair in front of a window where he could watch the birds. "He's more comfortable than he's been in months," his daughter observed.

Although these events seemed remarkable, no one on the hospice team was surprised at this outcome. When patients are prepared with simple explanations, reassurance, medications, and unrushed attention, an expert can painlessly remove a ventilator. This nurse, a skilled member of a ventilator removal team, explained that in her experience, when ventilator removals are done with adequate preparation and skill, most patients continue to breathe on their own, if only for a short while. She added, "It may be their way of saying, 'My loved one, thank you for finding the courage to free me from this uncomfortable machine. See, you didn't kill me; the disease took my life. Thank you for not forcing me to live on for months or years only to die on a machine.'"

Dr. Lucie's father lived for 11 days and then died peacefully.

As a physician Dr. Lucie was knowledgeable, compassionate, and approachable, someone you could talk to and trust. Her extraordinary understanding as to why she withheld hospice referrals for her patients was unusual and insightful. She acknowledged she had overlooked opportunities to introduce the *conversations* that would have prevented her indecision.

Dr. Lucie wanted to do the right thing and honor her father's wishes. Because she had no idea what those wishes might be, she responded as a genuinely conflicted person, fearful of making a mistake in judgment that she would later regret.

FURTHER CONSIDERATION

Many doctors would rather keep hope alive than tell patients they have no chance for recovery. Some fear that such devastating news could catapult a patient into despair, hasten a death, send a firestorm through a family, or earn the wrath of those determined to protect a loved one from the facts. It's no wonder some doctors delay delivering sad news. Even when news is bad, however, most people are grateful to hear their doctors tell them the truth about their illness.

If you or someone you love is seriously ill, ask your doctor to explain the diagnosis, the treatment options (including benefits and burdens), and expected outcomes. Even if you believe you have all the information you need, make sure that your doctor understands your goals for care.

When a doctor is unwilling to honor wishes, the best solution may be to seek a new doctor.

CHAPTER 12

The Pleasure Diet

M Y MOTHER LIKES TO SAY that all children need at least one person in their life who thinks that they are absolutely wonderful and can do no wrong. My grandma Daisy, my father's mother, was that person for me. Each summer I anticipated our vacation trips to the East Coast, where my more expensive food preferences were formed. I knew Grandma Daisy would greet us with giant shrimp cocktails served in cut crystal dishes on dazzling white linen. Just the thought of enjoying her fabulous meals and basking in her adoration still makes me salivate and feel her love.

When she was living out the last days of her life in a nursing home, I took great pleasure returning her kindness by sneaking past the nurses' station to deliver ice cream parfaits to this 94-year-old diabetic. After removing her untouched, gelatinous dinner, I'd feed her with a tiny spoon, enjoying her delight in the forbidden ice cream. When the head nurse discovered my sabotage, she squealed to my parents, who nodded in great sympathy and then conspired with me to continue to break the rules.

"What earthly difference will a little ice cream make now?" my mother said. "Grandma doesn't have long to live; she can eat whatever she damn well pleases."

Little did I know that even before I learned about hospice, Audrey had taught me about the pleasure diet.

I recalled her wisdom early in my hospice career when a nurse named Tonya told me the story of an elderly gentleman who refused to eat and was declining rapidly. When she asked if there was anything else she could do for him, he seemed to awake from a trance. "Yes, yes! A tall, cold beer, sixteen ounces... with a straw!" he gasped.

Quickly Tonya arranged for a doctor's order, then hurried out the door, heading for a neighborhood bodega, where she knew she'd find a cold one. After delivering it, she remained to enjoy her patient's sublime pleasure as he reached for the can. "Have you ever heard satisfied slurps as the last drops are sucked through a straw?" she asked me. "Ten minutes later that man died with a smile on his face."

In the last phase of life, forget special diets. My teetotaler, nicotine-free husband regularly reminds me of his last wishes: "Johnny Walker Red Label scotch, Benson and Hedges menthol cigarettes, and fudge, please." Years before my stepfather's death, he put in his order for French wine and cheese. Gabriel, one of his sons, fed him that last meal: a few morsels of Robuchon cheese and spoonfuls of Pomerol wine.

After months or even years of eating mushy, unidentifiable pureed foods, a favorite food can seem like heavenly manna. Sometimes, at the request of a patient or family member, a doctor will order "pleasure feeds" to indulge a person's special food or drink request, even if they have been on a strict special diet or are NPO (nothing by mouth). In such cases the hospice staff will explain that swallowing "down the wrong pipe" can cause choking or even pneumonia. That's why they teach family members precautions like raising the head of the bed and proceeding slowly with small spoonfuls.

Food preferences can change near the end of life. If a loved one rejects once-favorite dishes, experiment by offering different textures and types of food, whatever seems appetizing. The purpose of food at this time is enjoyment, not proper nutrition.

After her mother could no longer swallow, an ingenious daughter found a way to honor her evening ritual of a few sips of sherry wine. Each night she'd dip a mouth swab into a jigger of sherry. She dabbed the sherry on her mother's lips and around the inside of her mouth. Then she kissed her goodnight, tossed back the remaining wine, and departed.

FURTHER CONSIDERATIONS ON
FEEDING THE SPIRIT

Witnessing a loved one's refusal of food and fluid at the end of life can be distressing. As the desire for food diminishes in dying patients, the need to feed the spirit increases. Massaging hands and feet, playing soft music, praying, and offering a quiet, caring presence are all ways to feed with love at the end of life.

CHAPTER 13

Forgiveness

BY ANYONE'S STANDARDS, Jack is a remarkable man. Not because he took an extended leave from his successful business to spend time with his dying mother. Not because he came to the nursing home every day during the last four months of her life. Not because he brought her magazines, new clothes, and chocolates. Not even because he repeatedly, tenderly told her, "I love you, Mom." Good sons do all these things and good mothers adore them.

The difference is that Jack's mother seemed to be an angry, indifferent parent who felt no affection for her son.

When he said, "I love you," she turned her head away. When he brought her gifts, she spat, "I told you I wanted cigarettes, not this crap!"

"I admire you," I told him one day.

"Why?" He seemed perplexed.

"Because you visit your mother every day and treat her so well, when she barely acknowledges your presence."

Jack was quiet for a long time. Then in a statement of extraordinary insight, compassion, and generosity, he spoke.

"Don't get me wrong," he explained. "I'm no saint. My father abandoned my mother when I was a baby. I never knew him. My only memories are of her alcoholism and neglect—so bad that the neighbors complained to Child Protective Services, who periodically swept me up and bounced me in and out of foster homes.

"I ran away from her when I was twelve and stayed away as long as I could. I'm only here now because the nursing home called to say that she is dying and they need someone to make decisions for her." His bitter words seemed strangely inconsistent with the loving behavior I'd observed. But then he went on.

"One day I got tired of all my anger. It was eating me up, spilling over to my wife, who didn't deserve it. I made a decision to get help, to let go of my resentment, really let go." Then he laughed and said, "I've put two new additions on my therapist's house with all the sessions I've paid for.

"It's all about forgiveness. My shrink told me that anger and resentment can kill you as much as cigarette smoking or high blood pressure. She taught me forgiveness is a choice; it's a gift you give yourself. Even when there's no apology from the person who hurt you, you can still learn to forgive.

"This hasn't been easy, but finally I got it that this forgiveness thing is all about me, not my mom. I've given up my fantasies about my father coming back and my mother baking me cookies. That will never happen. She is who she is, but she's still my mom." He paused again before continuing. I waited.

"Actually, I did find some good memories when I was clearing out her apartment. She'd kept my baby book and pictures of me when I was little. I think she tried her best, and then life got to be too much for her. Forgiving her helped me begin to heal and let go of the emotional baggage I've held on to all these years. Coming here every day helps me in a selfish way because I actually enjoy taking care of her and other residents. If she had died before we reconnected, I wonder if I could have healed or ever forgiven her or myself."

As Jack's mother grew weaker, another little hospice miracle unfolded: it seemed that the weaker she became, the sweeter she became. She stopped cursing her son and began to melt the ice she had kept packed around her heart. At first she simply said hello and looked him in the eye. Then, little by little, she began to gruffly acknowledge his gifts and his presence. They didn't talk much, and neither of them brought up the past. Jack simply came and stayed and stayed until she died.

I asked my clinical psychologist mother to tell me what she thought about Jack. This is what she said:

Obviously Jack benefited greatly from his therapy. With help, he chose to let go of a lifetime of anger and hurt. What he accomplished is available to anyone willing to do the work even if there is no return gesture from the offender. Forgiveness is best traveled on a two-way street, although that is not always possible. Even in the dying time, many are unable to forgive themselves or others. Nevertheless, sometimes long after the death of another person, forgiveness is still possible.

I believe that Jack's mother never stopped loving him. Her rejection was a way of protecting herself from the overwhelming shame and guilt she felt for how badly she'd treated him. Because she could not forgive herself, she couldn't believe that he could forgive her. So convinced was she of her guilt that she was unable to meet his gaze. What feels like harsh judgment from another may be harsh judgment of self and regret for the pain we've caused.

Forgiveness takes on fresh significance when people know they are dying. Given two people who want to reconcile in love and forgiveness, old grudges can lose their power. Being right seems less rewarding than being happy, and achieving a peaceful death becomes more important than withholding forgiveness.

Jack was courageous in that he was willing to return to the source of his hurt and forgive. Offended people are more likely to become grievance collectors, dragging heavy gunnysacks full of rocks of anger and pebbles of resentment through life. They never learn that getting even and inflicting more pain does not heal pain; instead, it creates more anguish.

Actually, forgiveness is simple, but it is not easy. It can be so difficult that given a choice to forgive or die, many people would rather go ahead and order a coffin. To help gain perspective, I've often asked my clients, "On a scale of one to ten, with ten being dead, how important is this old grudge? Or, with so little time remaining before eternity, does this old wound matter?"

Jack was able to take the initiative and act on his hard-earned understanding and acceptance of his mother. He made a choice to forgive in full awareness that she might never acknowledge her neglect and abuse. In fact, it is rare for an offender to step forth and acknowledge guilt, in part because of protective denial ("It never happened"). The supposed offender may have forgotten the events or may claim a different memory of them. In such instances, there isn't much point to insisting on an apology or some other retribution, because such demands often deteriorate into heated arguments about who was at fault, who said what, and who did what. Although Jack's mother never spoke of their painful history, it was clear from their spending many quiet hours together that both mother and son had let go of the past to unite in the present.

Estrangement between people often follows offenses far less grievous than those Jack suffered. Indeed, when asked why they are so divided, many people cannot even recall the original offense. In some families children inherit their enemies along with their teething rings. What Jack learned and practiced can be used in anyone's everyday life. The Dalai Lama teaches that forgiveness brings happiness. Where there is anger and hatred, he says, the practice of patience and tolerance quite naturally leads to forgiveness.

People can learn and change until the last breath. You can't alter the events of the past, but you can make a last journey back to forgive yourself and others for being imperfect rather than carry such burdens until you die.

FURTHER CONSIDERATIONS ON FORGIVENESS

No matter what has happened in the past, forgiveness is always possible. When time is short and words are hard to come by, borrow the words of a hospice physician who suggests that his patients and their family members use a simple, all-purpose, last-minute forgiveness mantra, spoken from the heart: "Please forgive me, I forgive you." Even if you see or hear no response, you will be heard.

CHAPTER 14

Letting Go

"**I**F YOU DIE AND LEAVE ME WITH THESE KIDS, I'LL KILL YOU," my mother regularly threatened my father when my brother and I were growing up. What became an ongoing joke between them was, like a lot of humor, a cover-up for an uncomfortable truth. She admits that after his first heart attack, she feared the loss of the husband who met her deepest emotional needs. Moreover, her lighthearted threat was her way of telling him that she couldn't bear the thought of his leaving her to raise us without his strong and caring presence. "You two would roll right over me," she declared to my brother and me. She was right about that.

Letting go can be hard at any age. Most people don't want the end to come a minute earlier than it must. Also, family members are often reluctant to relinquish a loved one, even when there is suffering and no reasonable hope for recovery. On the other hand, some people, particularly those who are tired of fighting, signal, "I want to die."

Consider Monica, an 88-year-old woman, alone, in a nursing home, without family. When the hospice nurse, Will, visited her for the first time, Monica greeted him roughly, "I hope you have a gun in that bag you're carrying, because I want you to shoot me." At the end of a long life, she believed that she had nothing left but pain and suffering. Of course Will did not agree to shoot her, but he did assure her of effective pain and symptom control and a dignified, peaceful death. Monica never raised the subject again.

Another elderly lady voiced an emphatic no to her oncologist's suggestion that another course of chemotherapy might prolong her life. "I've had enough life," she said. Then, with a sly grin, she added, "Do you know why coffins are nailed shut? To keep the oncologists out!" Her good-humored doctor took no offense. Like many conscientious medical professionals, he hated to admit failure, to give up on his patient if there was the slightest chance to prolong life. Nevertheless, he accepted her decision, referred her to hospice, and remained her doctor.

Just as the dying person must accept and surrender to achieve a peaceful passage, those who remain behind must let go as well. When they don't, the ties that bind them to others feel like chains. Patients who are ready to die, want to die, and need to die may linger because a loved one can't let them go. When one person is so dependent on another for support, affection, and guidance that the thought of going on without the loved one is intolerable, the survivor may insist on continuing futile treatments or sustaining life support even long past the possibility of any human connection.

"I can't tell him to go; he might think I want him to die, so I said nothing," Sara confided, unaware that her barely conscious husband may have been waiting for permission to leave. A hospice nurse advised that she reassure him by saying, "It's okay to go. I'll be all right. We'll see each other again. I love you." As a result of that simple suggestion, Sara was able to deliver a different message and mean it. One of her children said, "I know Dad heard her. At that moment something passed between them. When she was able to release him, he was able to let go."

Contrast Sara's generous farewell with Eva's desperate plea to Martina, her 85-year-old imminently dying mother: "I need you; I can't live without you; I can't let you go. *Please don't die!*" Diabetic Martina's legs had been amputated above the knees. A ventilator was breathing for her, and she had a raging infection that originated from a bedsore. Barely conscious, she moaned loudly, clenched her fists, and furrowed her brow each time her bandages were changed. No one doubted that Martina was suffering greatly or that she was holding on for Eva.

Eva met with the hospice nurse, doctor, social worker, and chaplain to discuss the possibility of hospice for her mother. In one way or another each explained that her mother would not get better. "She isn't conscious but she is suffering" was the gentle consensus. They also reminded Eva that her mother's advance directive clearly stated she did not want her life prolonged by any artificial means if she had no reasonable hope for recovery, so removing the ventilator would be consistent with her wishes.

"No! The ventilator is comfort care," Eva insisted, then turned away. She continued to maintain vigil at her mother's bedside, where she repeated her litany, "You can't die; I can't live without you; I won't let you go."

Usually someone on the hospice staff can break through such a barrier of denial, but in this case no one could. I cannot tell you how this story ended because Eva surprised us all. She rejected hospice and took her mother home, where she and a caregiver provided around-the-clock care.

"What else might we have done? How could we have reached Eva?" I asked my mother. She responded, "Perhaps there was nothing more to do. Eva may have appeared strong and obstinate, but I see a desperate woman who hid behind an impenetrable fortress of denial. The only way she could feel safe in an environment that was foreign and frightening was by repeatedly saying no to every approach. This way she could escape the intimidating white coats and medical explanations she didn't want to hear. In the absence of a real enemy, hospice became the foe to resist."

Achieving physical comfort is a major goal for hospice workers; however, there are many kinds of comfort. Often it is not physical but spiritual solace that is desperately needed for patients to let go at the end of life.

"Of all the hospice patients I've seen, Anthony was the deadest," Divina told me. "His hands and feet were cold, his skin was blue, and he was barely breathing." With her unfailing intuition, Divina sensed that this man was holding onto life for some reason.

Although Anthony's brood of children loved their father dearly, they were eager to release him and to see his suffering end.

"Is there anyone else he might be waiting to see?" she asked the children.

"No, we're all here," responded Flora, the eldest child and family spokesperson.

"Well, then, have you released him to go?"

"Yes. We did as you suggested: each of us told him that we love him, and we'll miss him, and we will watch out for one another. We told him that Mom is waiting for him, and we will all be together again someday."

"Tell me more about your mother and father. How did they meet? What kind of people were they?" Divina asked.

The children chimed in to tell their parents' story. Anthony had been a seminarian and was soon to become a priest when he met Rosie. He fell in love with her, left the seminary to marry his Lutheran bride, and never again entered a Catholic church. Divina knew she was on to something.

"Has a priest visited him yet?" she asked.

A priest? The children looked puzzled. They were all Lutherans; why would a Catholic priest come to their home?

It seemed possible that Anthony was carrying feelings of guilt or fear of punishment for deciding not to become a priest and leaving the seminary and his church. Divina called a friend, a local priest, and hastily explained the circumstances. Acting more like the pope than a hospice nurse, she barked her instructions: "This man thinks he'll go to hell for leaving the priesthood and marrying Rosie. He's afraid to die. You must help him. Bring lots of oil, Father; anoint him on his hands and feet, forehead, lips, and any other place you can think of."

"Any other orders, Your Holiness?" The priest chuckled.

"Yes. Tell Anthony he's been forgiven and Jesus is waiting to embrace him."

Our sometimes irreverent Divina hit another home run. The priest did as instructed. Reconciled and reassured, Anthony took his last breath that evening. In telling this story, Divina mused, "I wonder if Anthony met Rosie at seminarian's night out at the burlesque club?"

Barely conscious, 62-year-old Mattie was admitted to the hospice unit of a local hospital after suffering a second massive stroke. Following her first stroke she signed a DNR and made it clear to her daughters: "If I can't get better, let me go."

When Divina left Mattie on a Tuesday, she explained to the daughters that all signs indicated that their mother would most likely die within hours. Twenty-four hours later, she was surprised to discover that not only was Mattie alive, but she seemed agitated and was trying to speak. Divina studied her patient. "Hmm," she said, "is there someone your mother might be waiting to see?"

Clarice, the oldest child, sighed. "Yes. Our brother Troy. He's her baby. He's in prison."

Divina moved quickly. She understood that Mattie might be lingering in the hope that she could reconnect with her son. Her voice resonating with firm authority, Divina called the prison, asked for the warden, and requested that Troy be brought to his mother's bedside. Immediately.

"Sorry, ma'am, that's not possible," replied the warden. "However, I will arrange a telephone call." Shortly thereafter the telephone rang. It was Troy.

Divina introduced herself and minced no words in explaining the gravity of his mother's condition. The conversation went like this: "Troy, I'm Divina, the hospice nurse. Your mother is dying. Usually I don't talk this fast, but we don't have a lot of time. I'm going to tell you in a few minutes what usually takes over an hour to discuss. Then I'm going to ask you to do some things to help your mother. Will you work with me?"

"Yes, ma'am," came Troy's reply.

"Your mama won't be able to talk to you, but she can hear you. She needs you to help her let go. I don't care how you say this; just keep talking. Use your own words; tell her you love her; thank her for being a good mother; tell her that you're sorry you've caused her so much heartache and it's not her fault you're in prison. Say, 'I'm going to be a good boy from now on.' Tell her it's okay to let go. Do you understand?"

A barely audible, "Yes."

"If you don't do what I've told you, you're going into solitary," she threatened.

Divina laughed and Troy chuckled with her.

At the sound of her son's voice, tears trickled into Mattie's pillow. Although she neither opened her eyes nor spoke a word, the deep lines in her forehead softened and her body relaxed. She had connected with her son.

Later Divina repeated most of what took place. "Troy was magnificent. He said, 'Mama, I've done a lot of bad things. I've caused you a lot of suffering... You were the one person who never gave up on me... I know that I hurt you...What went wrong was never your fault. I didn't call or write because I am so ashamed... I am sorry. Please forgive me... I love you."

Everyone in the room wept. Hearing her beloved son's voice, his words, released Mattie. She died peacefully that night.

For those who need emotional healing and peace of mind to die well, forgiveness and reconciliation bring balm to the soul: they allow us to finish old business and let go. Hospice offers countless stories of alienated people coming together again at the end of life: a long-separated sibling flies across the country to reconnect with a dying brother; an estranged child comes home to take care of a failing parent.

Even when such reunions occur, they aren't always successful. Some grievance collectors die with their resentments intact; some visitors carry their list of offenses back home again, still convinced that they were right and have been wronged. I have sometimes asked, "Would you rather be right or be happy?"

Although these stories focus on the end of life, letting go is available to anyone, any day. Now is the best time to heal old wounds. Because so many patients delay entering hospice until days or even hours before death, some already unconscious, there may not be time later.

FURTHER CONSIDERATIONS ON LETTING GO

If a loved one is experiencing difficulty letting go at the end of life, try to convey messages that will help bring a sense of closure: "It's all right to go. Your work is finished. We will miss you. We will take care of each other. We will be together again. We will always love you." These small but significant words can go far in releasing a loved one to die a peaceful death.

CHAPTER 15

The Last Hurrah

SITTING UP IN BED, hair tied back with a purple ribbon, Jeanne announced to her assembled family, "I'm supposed to be dying, but this is the best day I've had in a long time." Jeanne further astonished her family and the respiratory therapist by requesting the breathing treatments she had refused the day before while chattering cheerfully, "I'm supposed to be shutting down; maybe I should be shutting up!"

Jeanne's daughter Clare enthused, "Mom is getting better. Wait until you hear this: On the way in this morning I stopped at a bakery to buy Dad a slice of carrot cake and a brownie, because he misses Mom's baking so much. Before Dad had a chance to reach for the goodies, Mom, Our Lady of the Immaculate Table Manners, grabbed the cake with one hand and the brownie with the other and said, 'Carrot cake! Brownies! Just what I wanted! How did you know?' and proceeded to gobble them down. She swallowed the last crumb without a single cough. We were speechless."

Jeanne had been a master pastry chef. Although her delectable petits fours and pastries, artistically displayed on tiered plates, brought oohs and ahs from guests, she rarely nibbled on her own treats. Her joy was in creating them and seeing the pleasure they brought others. The family joked that the reason her doctor's office scheduled so many appointments was to satisfy the office staff's addiction to the scrumptious strudel she brought to every visit.

The previous day, suffering with inoperable lung cancer, tortured by labored breathing and a hacking cough, she'd refused even a sip of water. Depleted and weary, she had announced, "I want this to be over." Now this supposedly dying woman was laughing and reminiscing with her husband and children. What happened?

Actually, Jeanne was not getting better. Instead, she was experiencing an event called the last hurrah, a final surge of vitality that appears to come from nowhere and briefly energizes a dying person. People may get out of bed, ask for food and drink, and converse with friends and family. They may even consume a large meal that hospice calls "The Last Supper."

Not everyone experiences a last hurrah, nor are such events all the same. One man who had been confused and agitated for days quieted in his last hours. Deep into the night, he opened his eyes suddenly and looked at his haggard wife, who had been keeping vigil at his bedside. Lucidly and tenderly, he smiled and said, "Do you love me?"

"Did you ever doubt it?" she asked.

"Not for a minute," he replied.

She stood close to his bedside and said softly, "I will love you forever." A gentle silence enveloped them, and then he looked at her and said, "Kiss me." She leaned over, her tears bathing his face, and gave him a last kiss. He died calmly, quietly, soon after.

FURTHER CONSIDERATIONS ON THE LAST HURRAH

No one knows exactly why some patients enjoy a last hurrah. One explanation is that a final burst of energy provides a brief respite, like a long-distance runner who somehow summons the power for a final dash across the finish line. Families often consider this phenomenon a miracle. Hospice professionals think of it more as a final gift, a last opportunity to connect and say, "I love you."

CHAPTER 16

Extraordinary Events

M Y CLOSEST CHILDHOOD FRIEND, Julie, is nicknamed "Miracle Baby." Diagnosed with juvenile diabetes at age 12, she suffered increasingly threatening illnesses. By her mid-thirties it was clear that Julie was dying. She was legally blind and needed kidney dialysis to stay alive. Then something extraordinary happened to her that changed everything.

Julie recounted the events: "A blood infection sent me to intensive care, where my doctors and I thought I would die. It was there that I had a near-death experience. I seemed to float out of my body with a feeling of utter peace and unconditional love, relieved of all my suffering. I met spiritual beings who reassured me that death is merely a transition from the physical to the spiritual dimension. If people knew what death is really like, no one would be afraid."

Julie lived on to receive a groundbreaking pancreas and kidney transplant that cured her of diabetes and restored her eyesight. She also survived open-heart surgery to repair damage done by the diabetes.

Julie radiates calm as she continues to navigate a complex and often overwhelming healthcare system. Patiently she conducts her own research, processes the information gathered, and makes informed decisions in concert with her doctors. "I live in faith, not in fear," she says. "I am not afraid to leave my physical body because I know where I am going when I die. I am at peace."

I was new to hospice when I began hearing stories about unusual events. Moreover, I discovered that such occurrences are commonplace in hospice; no one is surprised to hear of another one. Those who experience extraordinary events may hesitate to share their stories. It is reassuring for them to know that such reports are heard and respected. Hospice workers soon learn to listen and accept whatever their patients tell them without judgment, without censure. Asking "What does this experience mean to you?" supports patients, validates their experiences, and offers them an opportunity to discuss what happened to them.

The stories that follow illustrate the diversity of events reported. Although everyone's experience is different, similar themes emerge. Most find their experiences enormously comforting and, as a result, they are less afraid of death.

When she was ten years old, Leesha returned from school to find her mother gone, the bed stripped, and her grandmother sobbing. Her mother, who had been seriously ill for months, had died, and her wasted body had been whisked to a funeral home, where the grandmother decided that a closed casket would protect the child and be best for all concerned.

All Leesha recalls about the funeral is the shiny brown box that supposedly held her mother and an odor that was an overwhelming mix of flowers, perfume, and damp winter coats.

Leesha's father had died when she was an infant. After her mother's death, her grandmother raised her. Questions about her mother usually brought her grandmother to tears, so after a while the queries ceased. Now, decades later, Leesha was dying of colon cancer, and thoughts of her mother consumed her.

During Leesha's illness, Divina visited several times a week, supervising her care and adjusting pain medications. As often happens, the two women became close.

"Divina, you never told me that dying would take so long or be such hard work," Leesha complained one day.

Divina nodded and waited.

"I'm so angry!"

"Angry?"

"Yes, angry! I'm still furious with my mother for leaving me. I've never gotten over her death. I believe I will see her again, but I'm scared of what will happen when I do because I'm still so mad at her. I know it's stupid; I know she didn't want to die and leave me, but I've never been able to get past my anger.

"No matter what, I love her and I still miss her terribly. There is even a part of me that believes she isn't dead and that she will come back to me. I never talk about these things because I'm afraid people will think I've lost my mind. Do you think I'm crazy, Divina?" Leesha was breathless after pouring out her heart's secrets.

"No, I don't think you're crazy," Divina reassured her. "You were a frightened little girl who couldn't understand why her beloved mother would leave her, who never had a chance to say good-bye." They talked for a long time that Friday afternoon, about mothers and daughters and the ties that bind them, about Leesha's anger and the emotions that consumed her. When Divina left, Leesha seemed exhausted but calm.

When Divina returned on Monday, Leesha greeted her like a child with a secret she couldn't keep, saying, "I had visitors over the weekend."

"Oh? Who?"

"My mother and a friend," she reported serenely. Leesha explained that her mother had appeared, accompanied by Dr. Martin Luther King, Jr.

Dr. King had been a symbol of love and strength in their home. Leesha's mother had hung his picture and told the child stories of his mission and courage.

"They spoke to me, told me that everything would be all right. In Dr. King's presence, that great lump of fury and fear I've been carrying seemed to melt away."

Once again, Divina simply nodded and listened.

The next week Leesha reported that her mother and Dr. King returned two more times. Then her mother appeared alone for a final visit to explain her fatal disease and why she had to leave so many years ago. She said that she had watched over her beloved daughter every day of her life and that soon they would be reunited.

When Divina left that day, she said to Leesha, "See you on Monday."

"No, I won't be here," Leesha replied. "Thank you for everything, Divina."

"So you'll be taking a big trip this weekend," Divina observed. "Is there anything you need before you leave?"

"Just a hug."

Leesha died on Sunday.

To Divina, a hospice nurse with many years experience, Leesha's story was in no way extraordinary.

My mother told me of a patient of hers, Tricia, a beautiful young wife and mother who became infected with HIV from a blood transfusion and then developed AIDS. At the time, in the early 1980s, the disease was practically unknown and there was no treatment. AIDS patients were seen as pariahs, isolated out of ignorance and fear that they might infect others who breathed the same air. My mother explained:

The entire medical community adopted a plague mentality. Nurses and doctors, psychologists, cleaning ladies—everyone wore protective gowns and masks in Tricia's presence. Her room was at the end of a hall; the door was always closed and carried a warning sign: ISOLATION! DO NOT ENTER WITHOUT PERMISSION. All that was missing was a skull and crossbones. Can you imagine how Tricia felt, shunned like a leper because of the common belief that AIDS was punishment for sexual promiscuity?

I can still see Tricia's crowded hospital room: The shades were drawn, the air heavy with moisture; medicated steam puffed from a noisy machine intended to ease her labored breathing. Next to the bed stood a bulky suction mechanism with a long, snaking rubber tube designed to pull out the thick mucus that clogged her trachea. In the corner was a giant laundry hamper marked CONTAMINATED. Next to that was a cart full of medications. Tucked among the tubes and bottles was a framed snapshot of Tricia, her husband, and their young son playing together on a sunny beach.

At first Tricia was bitterly angry at the injustice of her death sentence. There were days when she sent me away or refused to acknowledge my presence. When that happened, I'd simply ask her if I might sit with her for a while. She never said no.

Gradually she tolerated my presence and started to talk. She found a way to channel her anger into productive advocacy. Tricia became a national figure, an early spokesperson for education and prevention of AIDS. When she could no longer leave her bed, she used the telephone to carry on her campaign to educate legislators and the press—anyone who would listen to her about this terrible disease.

Then, in the middle of a freezing winter night, a hospital nurse called and said that Tricia had asked to see me right away. "My aunt Teresa was here tonight," Tricia said as I stepped into her room. (I knew that this aunt had died months before.) "She stood at the foot of my bed and said, 'Tricia, everything will be all right. I will be back in two days to help you across.'" Two days later, Tricia died. Recorded cause of death: complications from AIDS.

It seems that some dying people actually choose the moment of their departure to coincide with their loved ones' leaving the room. After I had spent hours at her bedside, my precious grandma Daisy died quietly when I stepped out of her room to make a brief telephone call. For years thereafter, I felt a nagging guilt for abandoning her to die alone.

The longer I worked in hospice, the more I came to see my experience replayed again and again. On countless occasions I've witnessed family members, cramped and tired from lengthy bedside vigils, take a coffee break or seek a breath of fresh air and return to find that death had arrived.

When I shared my observations about these events with a veteran hospice nurse, she speculated that private people often die a private death. Perhaps patients want to spare loved ones a painful moment. "Or," she added, "that may be their way of saying, 'I've moved on, you move on too, until we meet again.'"

Many other extraordinary events occur in the dying time. People once close but long alienated may come back together in healing and forgiveness. When families abandon their private wars and reunite to offer support and assistance to a dying person, little miracles happen. Quiet, respectful, in awe of this mysterious process called death, they put differences aside to express love in simple acts like washing a face, rubbing a back, or simply being a caring presence. I've seen people become more patient, more considerate, kinder. I've seen them acknowledge love never before expressed. Despite the sadness of the time, in the unguarded intimacy of the last days, many people are able to build new bonds and strengthen old ones.

The dying person too may express gratitude and love. Those who had found it difficult to convey such feelings may finally speak. One woman reported, "My mother-in-law and I always got along, but she never openly expressed affection for me. When she was dying, she took my hand and said, 'Rita, you are the greatest.' That was enough for me."

My show-me-the-evidence mother told me the following story that those who have lost a loved one usually understand.

For a few brief moments, not long after your father died, I actually believed that he had come back to me.

He always arrived home at about five P.M. His habit was to drive slowly into the garage, pause while he gathered his papers and books, then open the car door and get out. A few seconds later, he'd walk into the house. I liked greeting him with a kiss as he opened the door.

One evening at five P.M., weeks after he died, I was sitting alone in the living room. I heard the garage door open, heard the familiar sewing machine sound of your father's old Volkswagen. Alert now, every sense sharpened, I distinctly heard the car door open, then close. I heard his familiar footsteps. At that point I leapt to my feet and moved quickly toward the door. Neither frightened nor surprised, I felt a rising elation that filled my body like a helium balloon.

"He's come back!" I thought. Had he actually stepped into the house, it would have seemed entirely natural. I'd hug him tightly and we would dance with joy, ecstatic that he had accomplished the greatest feat of all time: he had defied death!

Now, is that loony or what? And this from a practicing psychologist. Actually, I've learned since, when trusted friends or colleagues feel safe to speak of such matters, that many people report similar experiences.

To a parent or a spouse who grieves deeply and wants desperately to reunite with a loved one, there may indeed come an eerie sense of presence that defies all reason. Many experts acknowledge that such events occur, but they attribute them to various causes. Psychologists might suggest that a dying woman like Leesha, who longed all her life to reunite with her mother, might conjure her parent out of her own imagination. Neurologists might track changes in brain chemistry that could account for the appearance of Leesha's nocturnal visitors. As for Tricia, her ravaged body, high fever, and heavy doses of morphine could have befuddled her perceptions. Aural hallucinations might account for my mother's experience. People of faith may credit the power of prayer or the intervention of a higher power with bringing forth such extraordinary events.

Not every dying person or surviving loved one reports an extraordinary event; however, many do. Whatever the cause, and no matter how different the experience from person to person, what seems a common thread in these tales is the peaceful, loving outcome. No threats or punishment for misdeeds, no more fear of death, just the reassurance that all will be well.

FURTHER CONSIDERATIONS ON
EXTRAORDINARY EVENTS

Reports of extraordinary events around the dying time are surprisingly common. It is possible that by inviting a loved one to share his or her stories, you will hear something that resonates deep within you.

PART FOUR

FINAL ARRANGEMENTS

CHAPTER 17

Funeral Plans

I MET BRENDA WHEN SHE DECIDED TO SEEK HOSPICE CARE. In addition to kidney failure, she had numerous other ailments including painful, golf-ball-sized sores throughout her body. She was paralyzed from the waist down, and her swollen body, yellowish skin, and sunken eyes spoke of her suffering, yet she greeted me with a warm smile.

After nine years of dialysis treatments, Brenda was fully aware that she was steadily losing ground. Despite the disapproval of her two adult daughters, she did something most unusual in the American medical system: she took charge of her own death. She informed her doctor that she'd decided to stop dialysis and all other tests and treatments and that she wanted hospice care.

Brenda knew that her decision was a death sentence. Without dialysis, patients usually die within days to weeks, depending on the amount of kidney function left and their overall medical condition. Despite the fact that she had just completed her final dialysis treatment, Brenda seemed relieved. "I'm tired of being tired; I'm tired of treatments that no longer help me; I'm tired of living," she explained.

As we spoke, it was clear to me that this courageous woman had a firm grasp on the realities of her situation, so I asked, "Have you made funeral arrangements?"

"No, but I need to. My two girls don't want to talk about it. Can you help me?"

"Ask them to visit tomorrow; I'll stop by and help start the *conversation*."

Brenda nodded, grateful to find assistance in addressing a subject her daughters refused to broach.

The next day Vicki and Annie, tense middle-aged women, greeted me politely. After the introductions, Vicki winced and Annie looked away when I said, "Your mother asked me to be here today. May I have your permission to discuss funeral arrangements?" No response.

"Go ahead, Susan," Brenda prompted.

What follows is most of what I said, not only to Brenda's daughters but to many other hospice patients and their families.

"It may be difficult to discuss funeral arrangements before someone dies, but it is important to do so for lots of reasons. Because she chose to stop dialysis, your mother will die soon. She will likely become increasingly groggy, then unresponsive and unable to communicate her wishes to you. That's why it's important to talk now.

"The moment of death is the worst time to begin making funeral arrangements. When your mother dies, you will enter a highly emotional space at a time when you need to come together and support one another. That's no time to decide on the type and cost of a funeral.

"When someone dies in a nursing home, the staff will ask you what plans you've made to remove the body. That call could come in the middle of the night. Right now, right here, you have the perfect opportunity for a *conversation* so you may listen to your mother's wishes, offer her suggestions, and make decisions together. If you do the work now, you will not agonize later. A single telephone call can get your arrangements under way." More silence.

I tried another approach: "Brenda, have you decided whether you want a burial or cremation?"

Annie, the younger daughter, started to cry. Vicki, the elder, cleared her throat and said, "In our family, the tradition is—"

Brenda raised one finger, wagged it, and said, "To hell with tradition! Annie, stop your wailing. Vicki, get your sister a tissue.

"Listen up, girls. It's a tradition in our family to wear your Sunday best at your own funeral. Not me. I want to be buried in that red satin kimono your father brought back from Japan. Just be grateful I'm not asking for the white satin nightgown."

"What white satin nightgown?" asked Vicki, obviously puzzled.

"Oh, I guess I never told you about that nightgown, did I? Well, when your dad was drafted in World War II, we decided to wait until after the war to get married. In 1945, when I knew the date his ship would dock in New York harbor, I took the next train from North Carolina to meet him. After three years of waiting, we wanted to get married right away."

Brenda paused for breath, and her daughters glanced at each other with "how sweet" expressions in hearing the familiar story repeated. Then they heard the part never before revealed.

"My best friend sent me off with a white satin nightgown for my wedding night. Your father took one look at that nightgown, tied it in knots, tossed it in a corner, and we got on with our marriage."

By now I could not keep a straight face, and the girls actually joined me in laughing. With the tension in the room noticeably relieved, Brenda got down to business.

"Buy the least expensive wooden casket. Use the same funeral home we chose for your father. I want to be buried next to him. Don't invite Aunt Sadie. She'll faint and steal the show. Everything else is up to you.

"That's it, girls. Now order that pizza they wouldn't let me have while I was on dialysis. Extra pepperoni. Let's enjoy every minute we have left together."

About that time I slipped away.

The more decisions made before a death, the less pressure survivors feel afterwards. Brenda understood that informing her daughters of her wishes would protect them from spending beyond their means out of a sense of obligation or guilt, or fear of being thought of as cheap. Brenda wanted a promise that her daughters would stick to her plans and avoid spending money that could go toward her grandchildren's education. Before leaving that day, they gave her that assurance.

Brenda died peacefully six days later with Vicki holding one hand and Annie the other. At the funeral, they told me they found great comfort in knowing that their mother's wishes were honored.

As difficult as it may be to plan ahead for the death of a loved one, often the bereavement time is easier for those who do. Also, no matter how much preparation takes place, it is normal to feel some regrets after a death: *I could have done more. I should have done more.* In time, such feelings usually fade in the realization that you did the best you could.

Initiating a *conversation* with a family member about final arrangements is a good way to keep everyone informed and avoid later disputes. Tell your loved ones your wishes and plan early to determine what you want at a cost you can afford.

If you are the person designated to carry out funeral plans for a relative or friend who never did and cannot now express wishes—such as someone with dementia—try to recall comments or *conversations* that might offer some hints. Hospice social workers and chaplains stand ready to assist with funeral arrangements. Many healthcare facilities offer such guidance as well.

In planning ahead, open *conversations* with your healthcare agents and family members if you desire to donate organs or tissues for transplant, research, or education. Include choices for donation on an organ donor card, your driver's license, and power of attorney for health care document. Some states have donor registry databases to document wishes in advance.

Have you made funeral plans? To start you thinking, the following questions may be helpful: Do you want an elaborate or simple funeral service? Where? An open casket? Closed casket? Cremation? A memorial service? If so, what kind of service? Religious? Nonreligious? Any special music or readings? A reception after the service? Where? What about refreshments? Any special food? Do you want a cremation and/or burial immediately after death or a service several weeks or months later, so friends and family have time to make travel arrangements? For a checklist of what to do after funeral arrangements are made, see Appendix H. See Appendix D for an important papers checklist.

Cremation is an increasingly popular choice. It costs far less than a traditional burial. Also, when cremation plans are in place, families have the option of having the body transported directly to a crematorium, holding it in a funeral home, or delivering it to a church for a service. If you are considering cremation, how would you want your ashes treated? Buried? Scattered in a favorite place? Kept in an urn? Unless you specify, you might end up on a shelf in the garage.

If you choose cremation, you have options to say no to expensive extras and services that you neither want nor need. Don't want to buy a glossy mahogany casket that can cost thousands of dollars? Don't want an expensive cloisonné urn or a specially constructed custom container? Say no. Ashes can be returned to the family in a respectable box at little or no additional cost. If a coffin is required for transport to a crematorium, specify the least expensive one, rent, or shop online.

Whether you choose burial or cremation, a simple, meaningful service can be held in a church, funeral parlor, home, backyard, community center, or park. A pastor, a friend, or a lay funeral celebrant can help coordinate the event. See Appendix G for a checklist on how to plan a memorial or celebration of life service.

Here's my mother's description of how she and my stepfather, Joe, approached funeral planning:

Joe had acute leukemia, and we accepted that he would die within months. After many *conversations*, we decided that while he was still completely lucid, we would make our plans. First we asked our pastor and a few close friends which of several local funeral homes they'd recommend. As it happened, everyone we asked praised the same funeral home because of their efficiency and the dignity of their services.

I called to inquire and learned that at no expense, a funeral planner would come to our home to help us explore options. I recall that visit as a surprisingly comforting event. The planner listened carefully to our wishes, answered all our questions about costs, but exerted no pressure to sell us high-priced services. Years before we had joined a burial society, which came forth with an unexpected generous discount. Asked if we would care to pay ahead and lock in a price that was sure to go up, we declined. Like everyone else, way down deep we expected to live forever.

When the planner asked if I would like to complete funeral arrangements for myself as well, I agreed because my wishes were identical to Joe's. Both of us wanted a modest, dignified service, where our pastor would preside and friends and family would have an opportunity to deliver brief eulogies. Our wishes would go on file at the funeral home.

After getting past the vision of flames and ashes, and in the conviction that we wouldn't be there anyway, we opted for cremation. And yes, we would take advantage of a reception room to welcome visitors and offer refreshments after the service.

On the morning of Joe's death, I notified the funeral home, explained that we wished to keep his body with us for several more hours, then set a time for the hearse to arrive.

The children and I washed his body, dressed him in his favorite nightgown, combed his hair, arranged him in repose, then gathered around his bed. Spontaneously, one of the boys began to sing "Amazing Grace." The rest of us joined in, some off-key, some with sobs, but with such feeling that those sounds still reverberate in my memory. For the next few hours we drifted in and out of the bedroom, saying our good-byes.

Carrying a collapsible gurney and clad in dark suits, the funeral director and an assistant appeared on schedule. With unhurried respect, they enclosed Joe's body in a bag, lifted him onto the gurney, and moved down the stairs to the back of a waiting hearse. Given the stresses and exhaustion of the dying time, I can't imagine how I could have managed all that had we not had the *conversation* or had our plans not been carefully considered and in place before he died.

Imagine a grieving widow or widower being asked, "You want the best for your spouse, don't you?" Many people later admit that they were shamed into buying more than they could afford or wanted. Under law, you are entitled to a detailed breakdown of every cost for any kind of funeral service. Get more than one quote. Compare one funeral service with another.

Whether secular or religious, held in an open field or a cathedral, every service has a place for ritual. Rituals are for the living; they offer an opportunity for people to come together to acknowledge their loss, to mourn according to religious practice or family tradition, and to find meaning and purpose in a life. Also, know that there is no obligation to hold a funeral service. Even where the mourners are few or none, a burial can proceed with dignity.

The trend for funerals is moving toward a celebration of life in addition to mourning its passing. I know of six sons who came together to construct a casket for their father, a marvelous creation fashioned of polished wood, festooned with herbs from his garden, and heaped with casually strewn flowers brought by mourners. That beautiful box even contained a mail slot for last messages. Old friends and family members greeted each other with tears, love, and laughter. Children ran up and down the aisles of the church; and anyone was free to take the microphone and eulogize the departed one. There were many stories of a real person, flaws and all.

At another funeral reception, a husband told this story about his beloved wife: When their car broke down in a snowstorm, no one stopped to help despite his frantic waving. "Get in the car," his wife yelled, as she emerged with a huge pillow tucked under her coat. She stood next to their car, raised a supplicating thumb, and the next vehicle slid to a halt to help this stranded "pregnant" woman. The laughter that erupted at this story gave others permission to tell their own stories of this generous, highly resourceful woman. What began as a staid, hushed luncheon became a memorable celebration of gratitude and sharing. As when silicon is sprayed on a stuck zipper, the difficult suddenly became the possible. Healing began.

While some people plan every aspect of their funeral or memorial service, others neglect to make their intentions known or to emphatically state that they desire no visitation, no funeral, no memorial service, nothing. Nevertheless, even when it is clear that the deceased wanted no acknowledgment of their passing, loved ones may still need to gather to reveal their thoughts and feelings and find comfort in sharing stories and expressions of loss.

FURTHER CONSIDERATIONS ON
FINAL ARRANGEMENTS

It is important to consider how you want your money and property to be distributed when you die. A will and other appropriate estate-planning documents provide a detailed road map for those who will be managing your financial affairs after your death.

Confusion can arise over the difference between legal documents that direct medical care and those that direct the management and distribution of money and property. While advance directives (a **power of attorney for health care** and a **living will**) govern your healthcare if you are ill and cannot communicate your wishes, a **will** and a **living trust** dictate how your money and property will be distributed when you die. A **durable power of attorney** appoints another person to manage your financial affairs if you are unable to do so. Because of ever-changing tax laws and the complexity of some estate plans, it is wise to seek the counsel of professionals who specialize in this area.

CHAPTER 18

Ethical Wills

A N ETHICAL WILL is used to pass on your personal values, beliefs, blessings, and advice to future generations. It is a way to tell your stories and share your memories. An ethical will is not a legal document; it is distinct from legal documents like a last will and testament or a living will. The practice of leaving an ethical will is an ancient tradition referenced in the Bible and found in many cultures.

What follows is an excerpt from a letter my mother sent me as she was preparing her ethical will.

> I started thinking about writing an ethical will when I was reading the novel *Cold Mountain* by Charles Frazier, the heart-breaking story of an American Civil War soldier. From my adolescence, I've read Civil War histories and novels and studied faded daguerreotypes of young recruits with ragged haircuts, in ill-fitting uniforms, looking fiercely into a camera.
>
> What engages me most are remnants of letters written by Union and Confederate soldiers. Using their words, I can create a movie in my mind and actually see these bedraggled, weary men poised on the eve of yet another bloody battle. Huddled over a campfire, cold, dirty, fearful of death in the morning, some drink for oblivion. Others wrap themselves in filthy blankets and curl up on the ground, hoping for a few hours of sleep.

A few sit apart, scribbling what may be their final thoughts and feelings on scraps of paper. Some of those letters survive. Written by ordinary men, some barely literate, they tell of worms in the hardtack, bad water, worries about crops unharvested and debts unpaid.

Others, the ones that grip me, write of the universal yearnings of youth faced with death. They recall memories of happier days, express love for a young wife or sweetheart, for children yet unborn whom they may never hold. Some express hopes for a future they will never know. Often there is a theme in these letters—a poignant desire to be remembered, to leave a legacy, a story of who a man was and what he might yet become.

Children tend to think of their parents and grandparents as people who exist for and revolve solely around them. Yet adults live other lives, often unknown to their children. My own parents were loving and generous to me, but other than a few brief stories, I realize that I know little of their childhoods, their inner lives, their dreams and plans, what they hoped to achieve, and what they believed they did accomplish.

How I would cherish a letter from my parents or my grandparents telling me about their youthful dreams and hopes, their triumphs and their failures. How did my immigrant grandparents feel when they left their childhood homes forever? Who were my parents before they became my parents? Once they were all young, full of life, eager to embrace the freedoms and promises of a still-new land. All that history is lost forever.

That's when I realized that something was missing in my will. I needed to say more, write something that went beyond that cold, dry, legal jargon, something more than the distribution of my worldly goods. I wanted to leave a written statement, a link to those who had gone on before me and to the generations that will come after me. I wanted my children and my grandchildren to know of my journey, who I was, what I thought and believed. Most of all, I wanted my family to know how much I loved them.

Whether you are facing death or have years left to live, you too can write a love letter to future generations. Writing skill, spelling, and penmanship don't matter. You can scribble on a grocery bag, compose an email, record your thoughts on a CD, or sit in front of a camcorder and interview yourself. What matters is content—your reflections on who you were and who you became. What were the events that shaped you? What are your priorities? Your guiding principles? What mistakes did you make; what did you learn from them? What essential truths have you learned that you can pass on to future generations?

If you hope to be remembered for who you really are, disclose that person. Don't assume others know your inner self and the challenges you met and overcame. Offer blessings, advice, insights, bits of family history that might otherwise be lost forever.

You might speak of what is good and admirable in each of your loved ones and of the gratitude you feel that each is in your life. Such feelings are rarely expressed, even by those who are closely bonded. In writing from the heart, you will discover more of who you are and what your true legacy is; you will come to understand how you have fulfilled your purpose and what you hope to be remembered for. Whether your ethical will is limited to a few scribbled lines like those of the Civil War soldiers, several pages, or expanded into a book, there is great satisfaction in completing your gift and ensuring its safe passage to the next generation.

Ethical wills can be written and revealed at any time. Some parents and grandparents want to share this information while they are still alive and can engage in *conversations* about the past. Ethical wills can also be used to explain why certain decisions were made in a last will and testament or to tie the loose ends of a life together for oneself and others. They may be written and rewritten, read aloud, or put aside to be read at a wedding, funeral, or other rite of passage like a confirmation or a bar/bat mitzvah.

"I'd like to do all that, but it's too late," sighed an elderly woman who had lived an exciting life as a missionary in China when I suggested she write an ethical will. If you feel too ill, too weak, can no longer write legibly, can't organize your thoughts, or don't know how to use a computer, enlist someone to be your scribe or recorder. Start talking, if only for a few minutes at a time. Talk it out over a period of a few days, weeks, or even months. Hospice volunteers relish the opportunity to help facilitate such a life review.

If you struggle to come up with words of your own, borrow from poets, musicians, playwrights, biographers, and saints. In doing so you may give others courage to examine their own doubts and struggles.

FURTHER CONSIDERATIONS ON
A TIMELESS ETHICAL WILL

A man who never left his little corner of Italy wrote a prayer that has endured through the ages. He continues to inspire people of all faiths who wish to follow in his path. His words embody everything he had learned and hoped for in his brief life, summarized in fewer than 100 words.

Lord, make me an instrument of your peace.

Where there is hatred, let me sow love; where there is injury, pardon; where there is doubt, faith; where there is despair, hope; where there is darkness, light; and where there is sadness, joy.

Grant that I may not so much seek to be consoled as to console; to be understood as to understand; to be loved as to love.

For it is in giving that we receive; it is in pardoning that we are pardoned; and it is in dying that we are born to eternal life.

— Saint Francis of Assisi

The Coversation:
How to Talk about
End-of-Life Care

W HEN I ASKED MY MOTHER TO RECALL how she and my
father talked about death and dying while my brother and I
were growing up, she replied, "It started when you were a toddler. Our
kindly next-door neighbor, Mr. Kenny, died suddenly, and Dad visited
the funeral parlor to pay his respects. He brought along your brother,
Greg, who was five at the time, in the hope of finding a 'teachable
moment.'"

Mr. Kenny was laid out in an ornate box lined in satin, with deep
pleated ruffles circling the rim of the open half of the coffin. The bottom half was closed.

"Antsy and curious but well behaved, Greg stood quietly, studying
the scene before him. Then he tugged urgently on your father's sleeve.
'Dad? Daddy!'

"Your father braced himself for an onslaught of questions.
'Hmm?'

"'Dad, do those ruffles go all the way down?'

"Stifling a laugh, reminding himself to answer the question asked
and not to overwhelm his little boy, he responded simply, 'Yes, Greg, the
ruffles go all the way down.' There were no further questions. Later we

realized that, for all we knew, Greg may have wondered if only half of Mr. Kenny was there!"

Ideally, *conversations* about death and dying start early in life and continue over time as the life cycle unfolds. In reality, this rarely happens. Most people remain uneasy with the subject of end-of-life care and admit they have no idea how to begin the *conversation*.

Opportunities surround us. For example, at a certain age people begin to scan obituary notices—"to be sure I'm not listed," quipped one man. The illness or death of a family member or friend, or a news story or movie can lead to a *conversation*.

After attending the funeral of an uncle who had been unconscious and on life support for several months following a massive stroke, Selena turned to her husband, Danny and said, "I'd never want to live on a ventilator like Uncle Frank." Danny nodded and thereby opened the way to other *conversations* that led to a discussion and documentation of their end-of-life wishes.

A single sentence can provide guidance. When Kim and her husband completed their wills, she asked him, "Do you have any special requests?"

"Whatever is easiest for you," he replied. When her husband died unexpectedly before providing further instructions, Kim felt comfortable making the arrangements she believed he would have wanted.

Grown children often must assume responsibility for an elderly parent, a situation that can lead to an uncomfortable role reversal. When Jason's siblings gathered for their elderly father's birthday dinner, they expressed concerns to each other about the old man's rapidly failing physical and mental powers. Just that morning he'd knocked down his neighbor's prized purple azalea bush while backing out of the garage, after he'd promised to stop driving. "We have to do something," they all agreed.

"Let me handle this," offered Jason, the eldest son. Halfway through the feast he rapped his fork on a glass, raised his voice, and said, "Dad, pass me the peas and give me your keys." His father's angry outburst ended all possibility for a *conversation* that day.

Contrast Jason's well-intentioned but clumsy approach with Peter's tact and patience. When Peter first invited his widowed father into a *conversation* about the old man's end-of-life care, he was rebuffed with a growl. "I'm not dying! Why the hell are you talking to me like that?"

"We're all going to die, Dad," Peter responded gently. "It's really not an option. I have no idea what you would want if you became ill and couldn't make your own decisions."

Silence.

Then his father said, "Turn on the ball game."

Respectful but persistent, Peter refused to be offended by his father's crusty resistance. Knowing that his dad might be more willing to cooperate if he believed he could lighten his son's burdens, Peter gathered his courage and tried again a few weeks later.

"You've always been there for me, Dad. Now I need your help. I'd rather that we have this *conversation* here, in the comfort of your living room, rather than at two A.M. in the emergency room."

Peter's father dropped his head and said quietly, "I think I believed if I didn't talk about it, it would never happen." Peter sighed with relief as the most challenging and rewarding *conversation* he'd ever had with his father finally began.

Like Peter, perhaps you have been brushed away with, "Yes, I should do that," or simply closed out with a firm, "I don't want to talk about it," when you've tried to have a *conversation* with family members. What seems like stubborn resistance may be fear of the unknown or of losing control of one's life.

Talking about other people's wishes may spark a *conversation*. For example, "Dad, Aunt Pearl told me she wants cremation. Have you thought about what you would want?"

Engaging in *conversations* about end-of-life care when a loved one has just been diagnosed with a incurable illness can be difficult.

"I can't breathe!" Mrs. Silva gasped. Earlier that morning, in freezing weather, she'd left home bundled in fur-lined boots and a warm, hooded coat and headed to a nearby beauty parlor to have her silvery hair styled. She barely made it to the shampoo chair before her pale face and labored breathing prompted her worried hairdresser to call 911. Within minutes an ambulance team arrived, administered oxygen, started an IV, and sped her to the hospital.

Her doctors agreed that she had cancerous growths in her lungs and that the disease had already spread throughout her body. They told Mrs. Silva's daughter, Joanna, "Your mother is not a candidate for aggressive treatments. She doesn't have long to live. I've asked a hospice representative to come and talk with the two of you."

When I arrived, Joanna immediately told me, "Please don't tell my mother that she is dying. I don't want to frighten her or cause her to give up hope." As close as Joanna was to her mother, she was unable to talk to her about her condition. She felt she needed to protect her mother and herself from an emotional meltdown.

I entered Mrs. Silva's hospital room to find a frail lady who greeted me with a sweet smile. After we chatted a bit, I asked her what she understood about her illness. "I've suspected for some time that something was wrong. I've had trouble breathing and I feel so terribly weak. I'm tired and I want to go home. I saw what my sister went through when she had cancer, and I want nothing to do with surgery, chemotherapy, or radiation. And I don't want to lose my hair!" she said as she patted her curls. Then she paused, glanced nervously toward the door, and crooked an arthritic finger to motion me closer. "I can handle this, but I'm worried about Joanna. I don't want to upset her. Please don't tell her that I'm dying," she whispered.

I recognized a familiar scenario. Family members often keep bad news from their sick loved one, who in turn keeps quiet to protect family members from the same bad news.

Joanna looked up anxiously as I rejoined her in the visitor's lounge. I repeated my exchange with her mother and before I could finish, Joanna exclaimed, with tears in her eyes, "Of course she knows. She's always sensed things. She's trying to protect me, isn't she?"

"Yes, just as you are trying to protect her."

Together we walked into Mrs. Silva's room.

What followed was the first of many *conversations* that led to Mrs. Silva's returning to her home with the help of family, friends, and hospice. She enjoyed visitors and kept her weekly hair appointments for as long as she could. Mrs. Silva died peacefully many months later, still in possession of her dignity and her beautiful silver curls.

Often a neutral outsider such as a member of the hospice or palliative care team can encourage and facilitate difficult *conversations* by offering guidance through what can be a frightening process. Even when the news is bad, overwhelmed patients and families often feel relief and gratitude when they hear the unvarnished truth. Honest conversations can be liberating because they end unrealistic expectations for a cure while releasing hope, a different kind of energy. Now, instead of seeking yet another futile treatment or consulting another specialist, many people are able to come together to take care of unfinished business and focus on quality of life in the hope of achieving a peaceful death.

FURTHER CONSIDERATIONS ON
CONVERSATIONS WITH YOUR DOCTOR

A white coat, unfamiliar medical terms, a hurried manner, and a beeping pager can rattle you enough to make you forget all your questions when you visit the doctor. What a physician actually says and what a patient or family member hears may be vastly different. When a husband asked his doctor, "How long do I have?" he later insisted the doctor said, "Two years." His wife heard, "Two months."

Write down questions in advance. Bring someone with you to take notes and provide another set of ears. If you don't understand something or need to hear it repeated, say so. Make sure you understand what your diagnosis means and whether your doctor will support your choices. Well-intentioned, well-educated, and well-trained physicians will more often than not resort to aggressive treatments at the end of life unless you tell them otherwise. Good decisions about your care are not automatic; it's up to you to make them happen.

How It All Began

THE FOLLOWING IS a bit of family history that offers a glimpse into events that led me to hospice and to write this book.

DAD

After my parents graduated from Columbia University, our family moved to West Lafayette, Indiana, where my brother, Greg, and I grew up. Dad became a professor of child development and family studies at Purdue University. Mom was mostly a stay-at-home mother until I started school. Greg and I joke that we were "bubble children" because of the Norman Rockwell feel of our university town and the protective love of our parents.

Mom and Dad were a tight team despite our best efforts to divide and conquer. They wrote many articles and books on family life. Greg and I were not impressed. We felt like bugs under a microscope when they gave us psychological tests, asked us embarrassing questions about our feelings, and included stories about us in their books.

Each evening we came together for dinner, family conferences, and general inspection. As our parents held court, I'd be slipping most of my dinner under the table to Capi, our poodle. Our long oval dinner table welcomed many guests. Often it looked like a meeting of the United Nations because of the many foreign students and lonely souls my parents invited into our home.

My brother Greg is an electronic genius. In grade school he and his best friend, Tommy, built a go-cart with some wooden crates and bicycle wheels. For power, he salvaged an old washing machine motor, scavenged every extension cord in the house, strung them together, then took off in a roar of triumph that lasted about 30 seconds—until the first cord came ripping out of the kitchen wall. Another time they strung wires between our houses so that they could communicate privately day or night.

Although my brother installed a doorbell on his bedroom door and multiple locks to keep me out, he was willing to hire me to bike to the local store for candy runs. My pay was five cents' worth of candy. He also paid me to write his misdeeds for confession at church. I was really good at that. My favorite one was "I was mean to my sister."

In high school, Greg pleaded to buy a motorcycle. *"No,"* said our father. That didn't stop my brother. Using his savings, he bought an aging cycle and hid it in a friend's garage until he could find some way to get past our father's decree. A few weeks later the friend's father called our dad: "Chuck, when are you going to get this damn motorcycle out of my garage?"

After the usual lecture and considerable negotiations, Dad relented, but with multiple restrictions, the main ones being that Greg would ride the motorcycle with a helmet, only in town, and never out on the busy highway. "Yes, Dad. Sure, Dad."

The next evening my parents and I were driving on the highway, and who should streak past us with an American flag on his helmet and another sewn to the back of his jacket but the newly christened "Easy Riker."

Greg survived adolescence. He's a wonderful brother, kind and generous and a lot like our father.

Our dad was a good and humble man who had a deep love for God, his family, and the underdog. He genuinely tried to see the best in everyone. I remember feeling uncomfortable and yet mesmerized when he would offer strangers standing in the rain a ride home. He called checkout clerks by name and always found something nice to say. I marveled at the reactions of surprise and delight to his kind gestures.

Our dad also was a great teacher. He dispensed his pithy wisdom to us in child-sized bites: "Never hit a child; it's not a fair fight." "Always eat some peanut butter before you go to a party; the food may be gone." "Teasing is a disguised insult."

He insisted upon good manners. I recall as a teenager skidding into his study on stocking feet and coming to a halt before his desk, certain he'd be thrilled to see me and eager to hear what I had to say. I asked my urgent question, and he paused before answering.

"Did it ever occur to you that you might be interrupting me?"

"No," I replied, clueless.

Instead of scolding me, he used that encounter as an opportunity to teach me to always inquire, "Are you interruptible?" when entering the space of another person. To this day, when I walk into another person's office unexpectedly or call someone on the telephone, I ask, "Are you interruptible?"

Our father assumed much of our everyday spiritual training with more of his one-sentence lessons like, "You know not the day nor the hour," "If you don't care who gets the credit, you can get a lot done," and "Always take Kleenex to church." To my dismay, he insisted that we sit in the front row at church. "Fewer distractions," he explained. I liked the distractions.

Dad taught me about humility, tithing, and anonymous gift giving. When we didn't seem to have enough money to buy all the things I wanted, I watched with frustration as he wrote what I considered overly generous checks for church or some charitable cause.

Dad also could be very funny. When I was a teenager, my parents took me to a conference they attended in Atlantic City, where I marveled at the sight of my first real Playboy bunny. As she wriggled past us, I heard him mutter, "Looks like they're serving filet o' breast today."

As a marriage counselor, he focused on the marriage, not the wedding. Years before weddings became media events, he helped young people to bring their expectations into line with the realities of life. "If it's all about the wedding and the honeymoon," he'd say, "what is there to look forward to when the excitement passes and you go back to the work of everyday life?" He believed that the right time to wed was as important as the right person. He urged, "Look for someone who shares your interests and convictions. Major differences are like fault lines that can lead to the earthquake of divorce when the going gets tough."

Because of my father, I became an amateur magician. When he traveled to lecture or to go to a meeting, he'd bring back a magic trick. In the summers when we drove east to visit relatives, he'd buy gum and magic tricks off the racks at Stuckey's restaurants to keep Greg and me quiet in the back seat of our green Rambler station wagon.

On stage at Purdue or as a master of ceremonies at some event, his performances were captivating. However, this charismatic man had his dark side: bouts of depression when he would disappear into the basement or withdraw for days at a time. In those periods, he was likely to go for overkill in accurately but devastatingly pointing out our faults. Greg and I dreaded the terrible moment when he would pull forth a list of our misbehaviors. He would tell us how disappointed he was, then proceed down the list of our latest mishaps and end with a lecture telling us what he expected in the future. We gave him a lot of good material.

Long before forgiveness became a common topic, my father was writing a book on the subject. Then he died of a massive heart attack at the age of 61. Only now am I fully appreciating who he was, how much he meant to me, and what a profound influence he has had on my life.

After I left home, I visited my parents every weekend. On the Sunday before Dad died, he was resting in bed, fatigued after shoveling snow off our long driveway. We were celebrating because I had just received a letter of acceptance to law school. As I sat on the bed, he took my hand and said, "If I never see you again, I want you to know how proud I am of you." I remember feeling confused and uncomfortable. Of course he'd see me; I visited every weekend. I was not to see him alive again. At that time I had no inkling that the dying often know the time of their death.

MOM

Driving home from elementary school one day, my mother took a shortcut through a neighborhood alley. "Mom, look at that!" I yelled as we passed a pair of giant plywood red lips sticking out of a garbage can. The car came to a screeching halt. "Quick, open the trunk," Mom shouted as she leapt from our little yellow car. Cringing, fearful that one of my friends might see us but lusting for that treasure, I obeyed. She grabbed those lips, flipped them into the trunk, and we flew down the alley. "One woman's garbage is another woman's treasure!" she said with a laugh, not the least bit embarrassed.

Actually, my mother had excellent training in Dumpster diving. As poor graduate students, my parents lived in Bancroft Hall, an old apartment building for married students at Columbia University. "We were all poor," Mom explained, "but life was rich."

Greg was three when I was born during their second semester at Columbia. They'd pass us back and forth at the door as one returned from work or class and the other left. Every Friday evening, like Little Red Riding Hood, Grandma Daisy arrived with a basket brimming with real meat and other exotic goodies.

Long before student loans, they managed with Mom working the 3-11 P.M. nursing shift at nearby Saint Luke's Hospital and Dad serving as a professor's assistant. "We knew that one day our study and perseverance would yield a better life," Mom explained.

Most of the student fathers, including my own Navy pilot dad, grew up in the Depression and fought in World War II. They were older, mature, used to sacrifice, intent on their studies, and determined to move ahead in their chosen fields. Except for my mother, most of the wives with preschool children were stay-at-home moms.

With little money for entertainment, the Bancroft Hall parents invented their own fun. For example, on the night before the city trash pickup, after people had placed their discarded but still usable furniture and worn treasures on the curb, a small cadre of students would slink out to go "mongo picking." Playful and laughing, the pickers would haul home their loot, trade with one another, drink a beer, and go off to study. "The pickings were pretty good," Mom recalls. "Once we found a stroller for you. Of course, it was missing a wheel, but Dad took one off the wagon we'd rescued the week before."

With all that basic training my mom can make a meal for four stretch to feed eight. She still saves a leftover ounce of grated cheese, only to pull it out of the freezer a month later to become the perfect topping for a delicious casserole. "Don't waste. Reuse, compost, walk lightly on the planet," she replied with a shrug when I accused her of harboring so many tiny "Depression cup" leftovers in our freezer.

When my parents graduated on the same day from Columbia University's Teachers College with doctoral degrees, the *New York Daily News* grabbed the story. My dad created a miniature graduation gown for five-year-old Greg, my parents donned their caps and gowns, and the photographer snapped away. A picture shows me clinging to my mother, head turned away to avoid the camera, while my brother, making faces for the world, revels in the moment. "You'll be on the front page tomorrow," the photographer promised. However, the first monkey ever launched into space took off the next day, and our family was bumped to the midsection of the *News*.

Mom was the glue that held us all together. Her energy, positive outlook, humor, and love bubbled around us. Whether she is wearing her horrible halloween false teeth over her own to smile winningly at the startled postman, or pulling a rubber chicken out of a pot for some unsuspecting guest, she loves to go for the laughs.

Once Greg and I grew up and left home, Mom would leave for her office early in the morning. After his first heart attack, Dad departed later to teach afternoon classes. His study was upstairs, and Mom was no sooner gone than our hyperactive poodle Capi would run downstairs and whine to be let out. With growing irritation, muttering dog curses, Dad would stomp up and down the stairs, letting Capi in and out, until finally he delivered an ultimatum: "Audrey, either that dog goes or I do." After a long pause, Mom inquired, "Do I have to decide right away?" "I received the dirtiest look your father ever gave me," she reported.

My mom started her professional life as a registered nurse and teacher and later became a clinical psychologist. She practiced for over 30 years or, as she says, "Until I got it right." She believes people have a tremendous capacity for growth and change, and she liked being part of the process. Retired now, Audrey remains vibrant and active, still one of the world's great listeners. Late in life she established a family foundation to help the poorest of the poor. The world is a better place because of Audrey.

THE CALLING

As a single mom working as an attorney at a family-friendly bio-technology company with a superb daycare center next door for my daughter, I longed for something more in my life. Then five things happened in quick succession.

The first occurred late one night in August 1995. After I put my night owl daughter Evelyn to bed, I picked up a magazine and opened it to a book review that highlighted volunteering for hospice. The article described how hospice volunteers spend time with dying patients to give caregivers a much-needed break. I read that article over and over. As I look back now, I know that is when I started to answer my call to promote excellent end-of-life care.

The second thing happened the following weekend when Evie and I drove to Indiana so she could spend time on her grandparents' farm and I could attend a high school reunion. As we headed home to Madison, Wisconsin, on a hot Sunday afternoon, Evie fell asleep. I was enjoying the quiet and thinking about my little girl starting kindergarten the next morning, when our car suddenly died. With no cell phone and no exit in sight, I rolled down my windows, put my head on the steering wheel, and prayed, reminding myself that courage is fear that has said its prayers.

Startled, I raised my head to meet the dark eyes of a man standing next to my window. "Hello, ma'am. My name is Angel. Do you need some help?" The kind young face of an off-duty trucker was smiling at me. Before I could respond, another head popped through the passenger window and said, "Hello, ma'am. My name is Dan. Do you need some help?" Dan was an on-duty trucker.

With the speed and skill of a road warrior, Angel arranged to have the car towed to a garage and repaired. Dan then invited us to climb into his gleaming 18-wheeler to deliver us safely home, via a truck stop for dinner. Evie was thrilled. Even today she still refers to our rescuer as "Dan Dan the Truckin' Man."

The next morning Evie bolted out of bed, ready for kindergarten. She was certain she had the best story to tell, plus we got to take a cab to school. She was 5 years old and that was cool. I was a single mom on a tight budget. That wasn't so cool.

Then the third thing happened. That same morning, in gratitude and feeling a nudge, I called the local hospice and offered to volunteer. I believe a calling is something our hearts are drawn to like a magnet. We may not understand how or why, but we can't deny the power of the attraction.

Despite my nursing degree and experience in the healthcare field, I had a lot to learn. I soaked up every word the instructor uttered. Frequently she reminded us, "Instead of the saying, 'Don't just stand there, do something,' when working with hospice patients, remember, 'Don't just do something, be there!'"

That advice captures the essence of hospice volunteering: be a caring presence; stay open and in the present moment for each patient. Listen, observe, follow the patient's lead—whether that means reminiscing with family picture albums, watching an old Bette Davis movie on TV, or sitting together in quiet reverie.

On Sunday afternoons, while Evie was with her father, I visited my patients. "Big Bess" was my first. She was a tiny slip of a woman, 85 years old and dying of cancer. Her 200-pound daughter and caregiver, "Little Bess," opened the door, slapped on a red straw hat with one hand, clutched a huge shopping bag that read "Welcome to Hawaii" with the other, and whizzed past me so fast she left a jet stream. I knew that she was determined to squeeze out every second of her four-hour break and that I wouldn't see her again for 240 minutes.

After I fixed raspberry tea with honey, Big Bess and I might watch football or I'd read to her from *People* magazine. During my last visit before she died, I recall feeling almost too exhausted to stay awake.

"Susan," she said, "would you help me climb the stairs? I want to rest in the sunny bedroom." In that warm and cozy guest room, the late-afternoon winter sun poured through the windows, lighting the pretty daffodil bedspreads on the twin beds.

"Now dear," she said, "help me to get into bed. I'm very tired and I need a nap. I'm sorry that we'll not be able to visit much today." She pointed to the other twin bed. "You just curl up there and take a nap with me."

"Oh, I can't do that," I protested.

"Please," she insisted.

Together we slept deeply for over three hours, my first nap in the five years since Evelyn's birth.

As I became more comfortable as a volunteer, I often brought Evie with me. She was like pet therapy. Patients and families delighted in her company and treated her like a puppy, with lots of affection and frequent handouts of cookies.

My outspoken little daughter was extraordinarily well behaved on these visits. I still marvel that she never whined or asked to leave. Evelyn is a carnivore of life, always on the move, taking everything in, quick to announce boredom unless she finds an activity worthy of her laserlike attention. She sensed what special people our patients were.

Evie particularly loved to visit Alva and Tessie because of their curly-haired mutt, GiGi. We watched over Alva and GiGi while Tessie ran errands. With advanced Alzheimer's disease, Alva could no longer speak, but I detected a twinkle in his eye each time Evie entered the room. A picture of Evelyn and GiGi still sits in my study. Both sport wide grins, and GiGi is looking up adoringly at Evie as if to say, "This is so great; we are together!"

As my Sunday afternoon habits became known, my friends wondered why I would give up the little free time I had to volunteer for hospice. The answer was simple: the rewards and satisfactions were immeasurable. I always received much more than I gave.

In a patient's home I became centered, in touch with my better self. If I arrived feeling petty, jealous, angry, or sorry for myself, those few hours always put things into perspective. My problems paled in comparison with an incurable condition. I always left feeling grateful for the experience, grateful for my life.

My stories are not unique. When hospice volunteers gather, the tales exchanged often focus on the rewards of service and the "little miracles" we witness. These days, when I address groups of volunteers, I remind them that if hospice stopped giving out paychecks, volunteers are the one group certain to arrive for work the next day.

Shortly after I began volunteering for hospice, the fourth remarkable thing happened. I'd read about it in novels, seen it on TV, joked about it, wished for it, yet when it happened, I didn't realize it for 17 years: love at first sight. When I was in college, my friend Kris invited me to a party in her hometown, Chicago. Across the noisy room I saw a gorgeous man: tall, dark, and handsome with piercing blue eyes, a salt-and-pepper mustache, and long, wavy dark hair. He was sweet and gentle, humble, smart, and funny. His name was Steve. The chemistry was there, but because of geography and other circumstances, it was not meant to be. Each of us married someone else, but I never forgot him.

Seventeen years later, two months after I became a hospice volunteer, Kris and her husband invited me to Chicago to join them and Steve for dinner. She explained that Steve was long divorced and raising his 11-year-old son, Joe. I felt like I was going on my first date.

Steve walked in the door as I was coming down the stairs in Kris's house. We locked eyes, and I had the same overwhelming feeling I did so many years ago when I first saw him. Not long after, Evie and I moved to Chicago and we blended our families. We took my dad's advice, went low-key, and were married by a justice of the peace. When I appeared in court years later for running a stop sign, the judge who married us also issued my court fine. When I reminded her that she had married us and we were still together, she let out a "Whoop!" that broke the tedium in the courtroom. A large group of scofflaws burst into laughter and clapped for me. She did not reduce my fine.

It was during my time as a volunteer that I knew I must join the remarkable, dedicated people I met on the hospice team. I made an appointment with the director of the hospice and asked if I might become their in-house attorney.

"Well, Susan," she said with a smile, "I hope we will never need an in-house attorney, but I do need a community liaison."

"What is a community liaison?" I asked.

"You would educate healthcare professionals and the community about hospice."

The thought of separating from my hard-won law career scared me.

"Would you like the job?" she asked.

After one deep breath, the fifth thing happened: I decided to take the leap and become a hospice employee. Once I joined the team, my fears vanished. My passion for excellent end-of-life care fueled my drive to educate anyone who would listen about the benefits of hospice. I loved my job!

ACKNOWLEDGMENTS

OUR DEEPEST GRATITUDE TO all those who shared stories, offered wisdom, and opened their hearts to help us write this book. Thank you to Kim Czarnopys, Dr. Wallace and Juanita Denton, Dr. Bruce Doblin, Steve Dolan, Dr. William Goodman, Charlie Garrido, Paula Lenz, Tim McGirk, and Dr. Clifford Swenson for providing feedback on the original manuscript.

Special thanks to copy editor Kathy Finerty and editor Dr. Kathy Landis, who provided invaluable advice and editing. Heartfelt gratitude to Tricia Crisafulli and Kelli Christiansen for leading us to Kaplan Publishing and to Susan Barry and Shannon Berning for welcoming us there.

Above all, our love and gratitude to Stephen J. Dolan for his unconditional support, from start to finish.

ACKNOWLEDGMENT OF PERMISSIONS

Special thanks to the following organizations:

The *Important Papers Checklist* on page 161 was provided courtesy and copyright of the Somerset County Office of Aging in Somerville, New Jersey (THE PLAN AHEAD PROJECT).

The *How to Plan a Memorial or Celebration of Life Service* article on page 175 was used with permission of About, Inc which can be found online at *www.about.com*. All rights reserved © 2008 by Kirsti A. Dyer *(dying.about.com/od/funeralsandmemorials/ht/plan_a_funeral.htm)*.

The *After Death Occurs Checklist* on page 181 was provided courtesy and copyright of the Massachusetts Commission on End of Life Care in Boston, Massachusetts. The Checklist is located in the Commission's End of Life Services Resource Guide at *www.endoflifecommission.org*.

PART FIVE

RESOURCES

Next Steps for Readers

PLAN AND PREPARE for excellent end-of-life care with the following checklist.

- Complete your advance directive and give copies to your healthcare agent, alternate agents, loved ones, doctor, and lawyer.

- Take a copy of your advance directive with you whenever you are admitted to a healthcare facility, and check with your doctor to make sure it is included in your medical record.

- Review your advance directives on an annual basis and after a major life event such as a marriage, divorce, serious illness, or death in the family.

- Initiate *conversations* about your end-of-life wishes with your healthcare agent, alternate agents, loved ones, doctor, and lawyer.

- When visiting the doctor, take someone with you. Write questions in advance and write down answers.

- If you are seriously ill, ask the doctor to explain your diagnosis, treatment options (including benefits and burdens), and expected outcomes. Make sure the doctor understands your goals for care. If you meet resistance, seek a second opinion.

- If you are hospitalized, ask for a palliative care or hospice consultation to help with pain and symptom management, emotional and spiritual support, and assistance navigating the healthcare system.

- If you have questions about whether to have a Do Not Resuscitate order (DNR), ask to consult with a member of the palliative care or hospice team. If you have a DNR and live at home, display it in a prominent place, such as on the front of your refrigerator, for easy access.

- If you have any other questions about end-of-life care, call hospice for a free consultation. See Appendix E for information about contacting a hospice near you and Appendix F for questions to ask when choosing a hospice.

- To ease the burden on your loved ones, plan funeral arrangements.

- If the above tasks seem overwhelming, seek the help of a trusted friend or counselor.

- If you knew you only had a short time to live, what would you want to accomplish? To whom would you express gratitude? From whom would you ask forgiveness? Is there someone you want to forgive? Who needs to hear "I love you?" No one can predict the moment of death, so consider answering these questions and taking care of unfinished business today.

Next Steps for Healthcare Professionals

TO THE HEALTHCARE PROFESSIONAL: Most ethical and legal dilemmas at the end of life can be prevented with advance planning. You can facilitate excellent care for your patients and their families with the following checklist:

- Encourage patients to identify an advocate, such as a trusted family member or friend, to accompany them on medical visits.

- Inquire whether your patients have an advance directive. If not, offer to help complete one or refer them to someone who can, such as a member of the palliative care or hospice team.

- Explain to patients how important it is to have *conversations* about their end-of-life care with their loved ones, healthcare agent, alternate agents, and doctor. If there is conflict among family members, ask for help from a palliative care or hospice professional.

- Make sure advance directives are on patients' charts and incorporated into their care plans.

- Determine whether diagnosis, treatment options (including benefits and burdens), expected outcomes, and healthcare goals have been clarified with patients.

- When delivering bad news, it is important to remain sensitive to each patient's support system, in addition to their psychological state, beliefs, and coping style.

- If a patient has a Do Not Resuscitate order, make sure all appropriate staff members know it exists.

- If a patient or family member has questions about whether to have a Do Not Resuscitate order, ask for a consultation with a member of the palliative care or hospice team.

- Secure a palliative care and/or hospice consultation when appropriate.

- Ask patients if they have had an opportunity to complete a life review and an ethical will. If they express interest, request help from palliative care or hospice professionals.

- Asking dying patients the following questions can help them take care of unfinished business: What do you want to accomplish? To whom would you like to express gratitude? From whom would you like to ask forgiveness? Is there someone you want to forgive? Who needs to hear "I love you?"

- In order to serve as a better advocate for your patients, and because no one can predict the moment of death, complete your own advance directive and have *conversations* about your wishes with your loved ones today.

Next Steps for Lawyers

To the Lawyer: Most ethical and legal dilemmas at the end of life can be prevented with good preparation. To facilitate excellent end-of-life care planning, familiarize yourself with the legal and medical issues involving advance directives or consult with or refer clients to lawyers or healthcare professionals who have such expertise.

- An advance directive is hardly worth the paper it is written on when compared to the worth of the *conversations* upon which it is based. Advise clients to open *conversations* about their end-of-life wishes with their healthcare agent, alternate agents, loved ones, and doctors.

- Instruct clients to keep copies of their advance directives in an easily accessible place in their home and give copies to their healthcare agent, alternative agents, loved ones, and doctor. Tell them to take a copy with them whenever they are admitted to a healthcare facility and to request that their doctors make sure the advance directives are included in their medical records.

- Advise clients to review advance directives annually and after major life events, such as an illness, marriage, divorce, or death.

- Explain to clients what a Do Not Resuscitate order is and how it differs from a power of attorney for healthcare and living will, or refer them to a hospice or palliative care professional who can explain the difference between the documents.

- Encourage free hospice consultations for patients and families who want to learn more about excellent end-of-life care.

- Advise clients to bring an advocate along when they visit the doctor—someone to help clarify diagnosis, treatment options (including benefits and burdens), expected outcomes, and the doctor's willingness to support the client's treatment choices. If the doctor does not agree with the client's choices, the best solution may be to consult with another doctor.

- If a client asks advice about a loved one who is seriously ill, is unable to communicate, and has not left instructions regarding healthcare decisions, consider beginning this discussion by asking the client, "If your loved one could sit up in bed for fifteen minutes and talk openly to you, what do you think he or she would say?"

- In order to serve as a better advocate for your patients and because no one can predict the moment of death, complete your own advance directive and have *conversations* about your wishes with your loved ones today.

Important Papers Checklist

Important Papers Checklist

_____   _____
Name   Middle Name

_____   _____
Name   Maiden Name

Residing At:

_____
Street

_____   _____   _____
City   State   Zip Code

Completed On: _____ / _____ / _____

Updated: _____ / _____ / _____

My Personal Information

My Social Security #: _____ - _____ - _____   My Birthday: _____ / _____ / _____
mm   dd   yy

I was born in: _____
city   state   country

My Religious Affiliation: _____   My Place of Worship: _____

My Father's Name: _____   His Date & Place of Birth: _____

My Mother's Maiden Name: _____   Her Date & Place of Birth: _____

I am: _____ Single _____ Married _____ Widowed _____ Divorced

My Spouse's Name: _____

My Spouse's Social Security #: _____ - _____ - _____   We Were Married On: _____ / _____ / _____
mm   dd   yy

In the City of: _____   Date of My Divorce: _____ / _____ / _____
city   state   mm   dd   yy

Location of My Divorce: _____   Date I was Widowed: _____ / _____ / _____
city   state   mm   dd   yy

Location of My Spouse's Death: _____
city   state

_____ I am a Veteran of the US Military   _____ I am the Spouse of a Veteran of the US Military

Dates of My/My Spouse's Military Service: _____

Military Branch: _____   Serial #: _____

My Personal Documents	Not Applicable	Description or Policy/ID#	Contact Information to Obtain Copy	Document Location
Birth Certificate				
Adoption Papers				
Religious Records				
Alien Registration Card				
Naturalization Papers				
Social Security Card				
Marriage Certificate				
Prenuptial Papers				
Divorce/Separation Papers				
Spouse's Death Certificate				
Passport				
Photo ID (ie Driver's License)				
Military Discharge Papers (DD 214)				
Veteran's Benefits Info.				
Other				
Other				
Other				
Other				

My Medical and Health Insurance Information

My Primary Physician: _____ Phone #: _____

My Blood Type: _____ Allergies: _____ My Medicare #: _____

Enrollment Dates: (Part A) ___ / ___ / ___ (Part B) ___ / ___ / ___ (Part D) ___ / ___ / ___

My Preferred Hosital: _____

My Medical Documents	Not Applicable	Description or Policy/ID#	Contact Information to Obtain Copy	Document Location
List of Doctors, Medical Conditions, Medications				
Power of Attorney for Health Care				
Living Will				
Organ Donor Card				
Medicare Card				
Medicaid Card				
Secondary Health Insurance Card(s)				
Prescription Insurance Card(s)				
Proof of Coverage (if not enrolled in Medicare B and/or D)				
Other				
Other				

Other Insurance Information

My Insurance Documents	Not Applicable	Insurance Company/Broker Contact Info.	Policy #	Policy Location
Life Insurance				
Disability Insurance				
Long Term Care Insurance				
Homeowner's/Renter's/ Property Insurance				
Automobile Insurance				
Mortgage Insurance				
Debt Insurance				
Other				
Other				

Beneficiary Information:

Name: _____ Address: _____ Phone #: _____

Name: _____ Address: _____ Phone #: _____

Name: _____ Address: _____ Phone #: _____

Name: _____ Address: _____ Phone #: _____

My Income & Tax Information

My Accountant: _____ Phone #: _____

My Income and Tax Related Documents	Not Applicable	Description	Contact Information to Obtain Copy	Document Location
Tax Returns (6 Years)				
Property Tax Info.				
Social Security Award Letter (Most Recent)				
Pension Check Stubs (Most Recent)				
Recent Paycheck Stubs				
Alimony/Support				

Expenses	Not Applicable	Description or Account ID	Company	Proof of Exenditure (Receipts/Bills)
Rent				
Utilities: Gas/Electric/Oil				
Phone				
Cable				
Home Repairs				
Vehicle Repairs				
Medically Necessary Homecare/Equipment				

My Property, Banking and Investment Related Documents	Not Applicable	Description/ID/Account#	Bank/Broker Contact Information	Location of Proof of Ownership (Statements/Certificates)
Deed to Home(s)				
Automobile Title/Registration				
RV/Boat/Other Vehicles Title/Registration				
Sold Property				
Appraisals				
Household Inventory				
Checking Accounts (including cancelled checks/checkbook registers)				
Savings Accounts Certificates of Deposit & Credit Union Shares				
Retirement Accounts				
Deferred Annuities				
Union Benefits				
Stocks & Bonds				
Other				
Other				

My Debts and Loans Outstanding

My Mortgage Company: _____   Phone #: _____

My Debt and Loan Related Documents	Not Applicable	Description/Loan#/ Account#	Creditor Contact info. Or 800-Cancellation#	Location of Statements/ Agreements
Mortgage(s)				
Credit Card Accounts				
Outstanding Medical Bills				
Owed to me List				
Loan Arrangement/ Notes/Receipts				
Other				

My Legal And Estate Information & Final Wishes

My Attorney: _____ Phone #: _____

My Financial Power of Attorney: _____ Phone #: _____

Power of Attorney for Healthcare/Agent: _____ Phone #: _____

Executor of My Estate: _____ Phone #: _____

My Funeral Home: _____ Phone #: _____

My Legal Documents	Not Applicable	Description	Contact Information to Obtain Copy	Document Location
Will				
Power of Attorney(POA)/ Durable POA				
Power of Attorney for Healthcare				
Living Will				
Trust Documents				
Funeral Instructions				
Pre-paid Funeral Contract/ Irrevocable Funeral Trust				
Cemetary Plot Info.				
Other				
Other				

Information about Advance Care Planning, Hospice, and Palliative Care

Aging With Dignity offers the *Five Wishes* advance directive. *Five Wishes* is a legally valid tool you can use to ensure your wishes and those of your loved ones will be respected even if you can't speak for yourself. *Five Wishes* is available in 23 languages and can be obtained from Aging With Dignity. See www.agingwithdignity.org or call 888-5WISHES (594-7437).

Caring Connections, a program of the National Hospice and Palliative Care Organization, makes free advance directives available online with instructions on how to complete them. In addition, Caring Connections offers other information about end-of-life care including hospice referrals and palliative care. *www.caringinfo.org* or call 800-658-8898.

The Hospice Education Institute offers information and education about hospice and palliative care, including how to obtain referrals to hospices and palliative care organizations and how to care for the dying and bereaved. See *www.hospiceworld.org* or call 800-331-1620 or (207) 255-8800.

The Hospice Foundation of America provides a variety of information, resources, and tools related to end-of-life care. See *www.hospicefoundation.org* or call 800-854-3402.

Questions to Ask When Choosing a Hospice

- What services does the hospice provide?

- Does the hospice accept your insurance and if so, what expenses are covered?

- Which medications, medical equipment, and treatments does hospice pay for or not pay for?

- What services are available to the family/caregivers?

- How many patients are assigned to each staff member who will be caring for your loved one?

- How often will hospice staff visit?

- How are services provided after regular business hours?

- How long is it likely to take on-call staff members to arrive if asked to make a visit after regular business hours?

- Is the hospice program Medicare-certified?

- Is the hospice program licensed by the state?

- What special certifications do staff have?

- Can the hospice provide references from professionals, such as physicians and social workers?

- Does the hospice provide short-term inpatient care? Where?

- Does the hospice provide services in long-term care facilities? Which ones?

- Who can be called with questions about care?

- How are complaints handled?

- How and why may hospice services be terminated prior to death?

How to Plan a Memorial or Celebration of Life Service

A MEMORIAL SERVICE is one that occurs without the body present. Celebration of life or life celebration ceremonies are newer terms used to describe this alternative to the traditional funeral service.

Memorial services may take place within a day or two of death. More often the ceremony is delayed for the convenience or needs of the family. They include many elements of a funeral: eulogies, music, prayers, readings, poetry, or other prose and symbolic elements to honor the life of the deceased.

Select a Date. Memorial services or celebration of life ceremonies are often scheduled days to weeks after the death for the convenience or needs of the family. Some may choose to have a celebration of life ceremony on the year anniversary of the death. A delayed memorial service can give the family time to plan a beautiful tribute to their loved one's life. Scheduling the service with a few weeks' notice gives out-of-town family or guests time to take advantage of airline booking discounts.

Decide on the Guest List. In addition to family members, friends and colleagues also need to be notified. Announcements can be made in a newspaper or by a radio station. Phone calls may be needed for out-of-town family and friends. Decisions made about an anticipated number of guests can heavily influence the choice of location or setting, thus the family may choose to have a small funeral service initially followed by a larger memorial or celebration of life ceremony later.

Choose the Location. One of the earliest decisions is whether the service will be formal or informal; this affects the choice of location. A formal service usually occurs in a church setting. An *informal service* opens up more possibilities for different types of locations: private residence, park, lodge, community building, or large amphitheater, depending on the anticipated number of guests. Other options would be favorite outside locations of the person – a beach, mountain top, or golf course.

Find a Clergy Member, Facilitator, Celebrant, or Master of Ceremonies. Members of a church, temple, synagogue, or mosque who plan on holding the service at their place of worship would have their clergy person officiate the memorial.

Other choices for leading or facilitating the service could be family members, siblings, parents, or friends of the deceased who are comfortable with public speaking. Additionally, professional celebrants can arrange a nondenominational service.

Ask Family Members and Friends to Speak. Decide how many people you want to speak at the service, then think about who would be good speakers. Choose family members and friends who are comfortable with public speaking to give a tribute or eulogy as a final farewell gift. Ask them to plan on speaking for two to five minutes.

Incorporate Other Friends and Family Members. Attendees who want to participate but may be uncomfortable with public speaking or too young can participate in other ways. Incorporate their talents into the service. Have them sing or play an instrument, read a poem, cook for the reception, or arrange flowers.

Other ideas include decorating the area, lighting candles, handing out programs or flowers, helping seat guests, hosting the guest book, or helping with food.

Plan and Organize the Service. In addition to choosing a facilitator and speakers for the service, there are many other choices to be made when planning the service. It helps having one or two people designated as the event planner or organizer to ensure that everything is done.

Being in charge of the service may be beneficial for some, giving them something to do during a difficult time; it can be overwhelming for others. Try to pick someone–family, friend, or professional–who can get things done.

Choose the Music, Musicians, or Music Delivery System. Music can help to set the mood of the service. Favorite musical numbers can be played as reminders of the deceased. A musical piece at the beginning and the end of the service provides structure for the event.

Music can be included in many different ways: performed by a soloist or a choir, played by a soloist or live musicians, or provided by a CD. Assign a person to coordinate the music for the event.

Choose the Readings. Start by looking for favorite poems, verses, passages, or readings of the deceased. You might also use inspirational letters or writings by the deceased to include in the service as a way of letting their own words speak for them. In addition, there are books and Internet sites with collections of poems, prose, blessings, scripture readings, and prayers appropriate for use in a memorial service.

Choose Flowers and Other Decorations. Flowers and plants are a way of decorating the location. Condolence flowers on display are colorful, visual reminders to the family of support from friends and family. Flowers can also be included as a symbolic ritual in part of the ceremony. Other decorations can be included: candles, fabrics, ribbons, and military items such as flags, photos, and medals. Memorial cards and programs, potted flowers or plants and decorative candles can be offered to guests as mementos of the service.

Incorporate Symbolic Elements. Symbolic elements can be incorporated into the ceremony itself: an empty chair, a vase of flowers, butterflies or doves released at the end of the ceremony, a candle walk. Gifts of memory tokens such as plantable cards or trees can be taken home by guests. The choice of symbols depends on the person, the family, and their belief system. The book, *In Memoriam,* by Edward Searl, offers many different lovely and loving ideas for incorporating symbolic elements into healing rituals.

Decide on Photographs and Other Mementos to Display. Single or grouped photos or photo collages of the deceased can be displayed to decorate the service. For a large ceremony, consider projecting photos of the deceased on a screen as a visual tribute. Amusing photos can add a touch of humor and be reminders of good times. Create a memory table. Invite family and friends to bring photos and other mementos: newspaper clippings, awards, artwork, writing, and symbols of the deceased's favorite hobbies.

Determine the Food and Refreshments. Sharing food during times of bereavement is an ancient practice that still remains popular. Food and refreshments can range from light refreshments to potlucks, seated luncheons, or elaborate catered dinners. Include some of the deceased's favorite foods in the menu. Distraught emotions and alcohol are a bad combination. Serve water, punch, tea, or coffee instead.

Find a Way to Share Memories. Encourage attendees to write down a favorite memory beforehand that can be shared at the service. Have an extra copy available for the family. Consider allowing time for an open microphone for the people who are not scheduled to speak but still want to share their remembrances.

Find a Way to Preserve Memories. Provide formal guest books for attendees to sign. Having more than one book cuts down on the time spent waiting in line.

Pass out index cards or printed note cards and have attendees write down their memories: "I'll always remember the time when..." or "I wish I'd had the chance to say..." These cards can be stored and shared later to preserve the memories of the loved one's friends from the day of the service.

After Death Occurs Checklist

SPECIAL THANKS *to the Massachusetts Commission on End of Life Care for granting permission to use an adapted version of the After Death Occurs Checklist located in the Commission's End of Life Services Resource Guide. See www.endoflifecommission.org.*

The time immediately following the death of a loved one can be overwhelming, with grief and bereavement complicated by a seemingly endless number of tasks. The immediate days following the death will be focused on the funeral or memorial service arrangements. Soon after, however, various financial and legal issues must be addressed. Many people find it difficult to be sure they have taken care of everything. The following is a list of tasks that are likely to need attention:

❑ **Call the funeral home** you have selected. If you have not chosen a funeral home, ask a friend, family member, or clergy for a reference to a local funeral home.

❑ **If your loved one was a veteran,** you may be able to get assistance with the funeral, burial plot, or other benefits. For information on benefits, call the Veterans Administration at 800-827-1000. You will need a copy of your loved one's discharge papers.

❑ **Obtain 10 to 15 copies of the death certificate** from your funeral director.

❑ If your loved one was receiving Social Security benefits, **notify your local Social Security office** of the death, since these benefits will stop. Overpayments will result in a difficult process of repayment. If you are a surviving spouse, ask about your eligibility for increased benefits. Also check on benefits that any minor children may be entitled to receive.

❑ **Contact the health insurance company or employer** regarding terminating coverage for the deceased while continuing coverage for others covered through the policy.

❑ **Contact the insurance company** for all life insurance policies. You will need to provide the policy number and a certified copy of the death certificate and fill out a claim form. If the deceased is listed as the beneficiary on any other policy, arrange to have the name removed.

❑ If the deceased was working, **contact the employer for information** on pension plans, credit unions, and union death benefits. You will need a certified copy of the death certificate for each claim.

❏ **Return credit cards of the deceased** with a certified copy of the death certificate, or notify the credit card company if you, as the survivor, want to retain use of the card.

❏ **Seek the advice of an accountant or tax advisor** about filing the deceased's tax return for the year of the death. Keep monthly bank statements on all individual and joint accounts that show the account balance on the day of death, since you will need this information for the estate tax return.

❏ **Arrange to change any joint bank accounts into your name.** If the deceased's estate is in trust, check with the trust department or customer service at the bank.

❏ **If the deceased owned a car,** transfer the automobile title into your name at the secretary of state's office, or if the estate is probated, through probate court.

❏ **Arrange to change stocks and bonds into your name.** Your bank or stockbroker will have the forms.

❏ **Make sure that important bills,** such as mortgage payments, continue to be paid.

Documents you may need to complete the tasks:

• Death certificates (10 to 15 certified copies)

• Social Security card

• Marriage certificate

• Birth certificate

• Birth certificate for each child, if applicable

• Insurance policies

• Deed and titles to property

- Stock certificates

- Bank books

- Honorable discharge papers for a veteran and/or V.A. claim number

- Recent income tax forms and W-2 forms

- Automobile title and registration papers

- Loan and installment payment books and/or contracts

ABOUT THE AUTHORS

Susan Riker Dolan, RN, JD, is a registered nurse and an attorney. Susan practiced healthcare and corporate law and is licensed as an attorney and nurse in Indiana, Illinois and Wisconsin. She served as executive director for a national hospice organization, is a healthcare consultant and a broadcast host for satellite radio station ReachMD XM 157, the channel for medical professionals. For more information, or to contact the authors, see *www.susandolan.com*

Audrey Riker Vizzard, RN, EdD, is a nurse and clinical psychologist. She is a former adjunct professor of psychology at Purdue University and the author of many books and articles. She served as a hospice volunteer and facilitates an ongoing Good Grief Group for seniors actively dealing with care giving and loss. Audrey also serves as the director of her family foundation.